MATT CHRISTOPHER®

On the Field with...

Alex Rodriguez

Text by Glenn Stout

WITHDRAWN

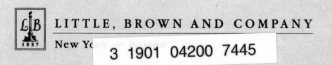

LITTLE, BROWN AND COMPANY

New York

Little, Brown and Company

Hachette Book Group USA
1271 Avenue of Americas, New York, NY 10020
Visit our Web site at www.lb-kids.com

www.mattchristopher.com

First Edition

Matt Christopher® is a registered trademark of Matt Christopher Royalties, Inc.

Cover photograph by Tom DiPace

Library of Congress Cataloging-in-Publication Data

Stout, Glenn.
    On the field with — Alex Rodriguez / text by Glenn Stout. — 1st ed.
        p.   cm.
    Summary: A biography of the talented Seattle Mariners' shortstop, Alex Rodriguez, who signed with the Texas Rangers for the 2001 season.
    ISBN 0-316-14483-5
    1. Rodriguez, Alex, 1975–   — Juvenile literature.   2. Baseball players — United States — Biography — Juvenile literature.
    [1. Rodriguez, Alex, 1975–   2. Baseball players.   3. Dominican Americans — Biography.]   I. Title. At head of title: Matt Christopher.
    II. Christopher, Matt.   III. Title.
    GV865.R62 S86   2001
    796.357'092
    [B] — dc21   2001034449

10 9 8 7 6 5 4

COM-MO

Printed in the United States of America

Contents

Chapter One:
1975–1984

Son of the Dominican

One summer day in the Dominican Republic, a small island country in the Caribbean, a group of young boys were playing baseball at the local *monte*, the Spanish word for "park."

Most of the boys were nine or ten years old. They shared a single, yellow aluminum bat. The ball they used was worn and wrapped with tape.

Friends and family surrounded the makeshift diamond, yelling words of encouragement. The smallest and youngest boy on the field, a six-year-old named Alex, stepped to the plate.

Alex didn't care that the field looked nothing like a real baseball field. Even though the grass was worn down and none of the players wore a real uniform, in Alex's imagination he was in a major league ball-park and he was a major league baseball player.

Some of the older players laughed and hooted at the young boy. Not only was he small, he was also a newcomer who had recently moved to the Dominican from the United States. He didn't speak Spanish as well as the other boys and hadn't made many friends. Most of the players didn't think a boy so young and so small even belonged in the game.

When the boy stepped up to the plate, the only words he paid attention to were the supportive calls of his parents. He heard their voices, but he didn't turn and look their way. With a serious expression on his face he stared hard at the pitcher and waved the bat, curling it back over his shoulder and concentrating.

The pitcher didn't want the little player with the yellow bat to get a hit and embarrass him. He wound up and threw the ball as hard as he could.

The little boy clenched his teeth, and as the ball approached the plate he took a long, level swing.

"Pow!"

The old ball rocketed off the bat, over the head of

the third baseman, and down the left-field line toward a distant corner of the *monte*. Alex threw his bat to the ground and began running as fast as he could toward first base.

He scampered around the bases as the crowd cheered and the left fielder chased after the bounding ball. By the time the outfielder retrieved it, the little boy had rounded second base and was running hard toward third. As the fielder threw the ball in toward the infield, the little boy was on his way to home plate. The shortstop caught the relay, spun, and threw home in one motion.

But he was too late. Exhausted and breathing heavily, Alex crossed home plate just before the ball arrived.

Home run!

His teammates surrounded him and pounded on his back. His parents cheered and smiled proudly. The pitcher frowned and pounded his glove. As the little boy recalled years later, "I was almost crying, I was so happy."

Alex Rodriguez had just hit the very first home run of his life. Over the years, as the little boy grew into a man, the scene would be repeated time and time again. Today, when Texas Ranger shortstop Alex Rodriguez hits a home run, he still remembers that day so long ago in the Dominican Republic.

And when Alex Rodriguez hits a home run or does anything else on a baseball field, he is still happy. Playing baseball has always been one thing in his life that has made Alex Rodriguez happy. As his mother later recalled, from the moment he picked up a plastic baseball bat at age two, all Alex ever wanted to do was become a baseball player.

"He was very focused from the time he was a child and just wasn't interested in anything else," she said. "He didn't care about the sun or the rain. He just had to play ball and would cry if I didn't take him to the park every day."

Alex Rodriguez has very few reasons to cry today. After becoming a star shortstop for the Seattle Mariners, he signed a new contract in 2001 worth 252 million dollars to play for the Texas Rangers. He gets to go to the ballpark every day and do what he enjoys most. At an age when most baseball players are still trying to make it in the major leagues, Alex is considered one of the best players in the game today.

But Rodriguez didn't find such happiness easy to attain. He has worked hard for everything he has achieved. If not for baseball and the help of some very special people, his life may have turned out quite differently.

Alex was born in New York City on July 27, 1975. His father, Victor, owned a successful shoe store and his mother, Lourdes, showered Alex with love and attention.

He was the baby of the family. His sister, Susy, and brother, Joe, were already grown up and living away from home when Alex was born.

His parents had met and married in the Dominican Republic. Even though the Dominican Republic is a very poor country, they were proud of their heritage.

Life is hard in the Dominican. Jobs are few, and many Dominicans have to struggle to make a living, working hard for a few dollars a day. Average people earn less than $1,000 a year. But they still have dreams of success.

Many Dominicans dream of moving to the United States and making a better life for themselves. For many Dominican boys and young men, that dream includes playing the game of baseball.

That was Victor Rodriguez's dream, too. He loved baseball.

Baseball is perhaps more popular in the Dominican Republic than anywhere else in the world. The game was brought to the country late in the nineteenth century. Factory owners and the men who owned large agricultural plantations began sponsoring teams to provide entertainment for their workers.

It is warm and sunny nearly all of the time in the Dominican, and it is possible to play baseball all year long. The game quickly became very popular, and soon Dominican players were among the very best in the world, equal in talent to those who played major league baseball in the United States.

But many Dominican players were not allowed to play major league baseball in the United States. Most Dominicans were multiracial, and their ancestors include African slaves who were brought to the

Dominican to work in the fields. Until 1947, when Jackie Robinson began playing for the Brooklyn Dodgers, major league baseball did not allow people of African descent to play. The game was segregated. Only white players were allowed to compete.

That didn't stop Dominicans from playing the game. A few even made their way to the United States and played in the Negro Leagues. After a professional league began in the Dominican, some Negro Leaguers even traveled to the Dominican Republic to play professional baseball there.

After Jackie Robinson broke the color barrier in the United States, American baseball scouts began looking for players in the Dominican. Many of the best Dominican players eventually made their way to the major leagues, like star pitcher Juan Marichal, who became the first Dominican ballplayer named to the Baseball Hall of Fame. And American players, both white and black, started traveling to the Dominican to play in the winter league.

Victor Rodriguez was a good baseball player. A catcher, he played in the Dominican professional league. But he wasn't talented enough to play in the major leagues. He stopped playing and went to work.

After he married Lourdes, he decided to move to the United States to make a better life for his family. He had relatives in New York City.

They settled in Washington Heights, a New York neighborhood where many Dominicans live. Victor and Lourdes worked hard and saved their money. Eventually, Victor opened a shoe store.

The shoe store was more successful than Victor ever dreamed it would be. He was able to make a comfortable life for his family. After Alex was born in 1975, Victor began thinking about the future.

He was tired of working long hours every day. And he missed the Dominican Republic.

So when Alex was four years old, Victor decided to retire and return the family to the Dominican Republic. He turned his shoe store over to some relatives. They would run the store and send some of the profits to the Rodriguezes in the Dominican. Although the family wasn't rich, they had enough money to live comfortably in the Dominican. They lived in a large house less than a mile from the beach and even had a maid to help with housework.

Like most other Dominican boys, little Alex was introduced to baseball at a young age. In the Dominican, boys play baseball in virtually every park or empty lot. Although they often lack proper equipment, like gloves and new baseballs, the players make up for that with their enthusiasm. Many boys play baseball almost all day long all year round.

Except when he was in school, that's what Alex Rodriguez did. His father encouraged him to play and helped him practice. By the time he was six years old, Alex was talented enough to play with boys three or four years older. He could run fast and throw the ball accurately. At an age when many American boys are still learning to hit from a batting tee, Alex could hit baseballs thrown by a pitcher.

But when Alex was eight years old, the family received some bad news. Without Victor Rodriguez to run the business, the shoe store in New York wasn't doing very well. He would have to go back to work.

He decided to take the family and return to the

United States. They moved to Kendall, Florida, just outside Miami. Victor opened a new store, once again working long hours to make it succeed.

It was a big change for Alex, but he adapted quickly. There are many Latino people in Miami, and Alex fit right in, speaking both English and Spanish. He went to school and kept playing baseball, participating in local youth leagues. His parents often watched him play, and each time Alex got a hit or made a nice play, his father beamed with pride. But shortly after Alex celebrated his ninth birthday, his life changed dramatically.

Victor Rodriguez left home one day and never returned. Alex, his sister, brother, and mother were on their own.

Chapter Two:
1984–1991

Making It in Miami

Alex didn't understand why his father left. He later said to a reporter, "What did I know back then? I thought he was coming back. I thought that he had gone to the store or something. But he never came back."

Alex found out many years later that Victor hadn't liked Miami. He wanted to move the family back to New York, but his wife had disagreed. So he left them behind and returned to New York himself.

"He had been so good to me, actually spoiled me because I was the baby of the family," remembers Alex. "I couldn't understand what he had done. To this day, I still don't know how a man could do that to his family: turn his back."

Alex had to grow up fast. His mother went to work in an office and sometimes moonlighted as a waitress. His sister, Susy, and brother, Joe, took over a larger role in his life to make up for the absence of his father. They set a good example. Both had gone to college. Susy eventually earned a law degree, and Joe became a businessman.

Alex would later call Susy the "secretary of education." While his mother was working, Susy always made sure Alex went to school and did his homework. Joe became the "secretary of sports." He made sure Alex learned to play the right way.

But it was still hard for Alex. "I lied to myself," he later recalled. "I tried to tell myself it didn't matter. But when I was alone, I often cried. Where was my father?"

Alex was fortunate. After his father left, there were still plenty of people who cared about him. His best friend was a boy named J. D. Arteaga. When J. D.'s father learned that Alex's father had left the family, he took an interest in the young boy. Mr. Arteaga listened patiently to Alex's troubles and tried to teach him the right way to behave and live his life. "He was like my second father," Alex once said.

Alex and J. D. were inseparable. They played together on the same team sponsored by the Boys Club. Alex usually played shortstop, but when J. D. pitched, Alex caught.

Mr. Arteaga realized that Alex, like his own son, loved baseball more than anything else. One day he told young Alex, "You are a great ballplayer. You are going a long way, and I'm going to take you there." Mr. Arteaga became Alex's first baseball coach.

Alex also found some help at the Hank Kline Boys and Girls Club in Miami. He would often go there to play with his friends after school. A man who worked at the Boys Club, Eddie "Gallo" Rodriguez, became one of Alex's mentors and, later, one of his best friends.

Alex loved hearing his stories. Rodriguez had played several years of minor league baseball and he spent hours working with Alex, teaching him how to play. He told Alex that major league baseball players

Jose Canseco and Rafael Palmeiro had been members of the Boys and Girls Club when they were kids.

That made an impression on Alex. Like many other kids, Alex followed major-league baseball. His favorite player was Baltimore Oriole shortstop Cal Ripken.

Ripken is often credited with revolutionizing the way the shortstop position is perceived. Before Ripken reached the major leagues in 1981, shortstops were expected to be good fielders and little more. Their ability to hit was considered a bonus. Most shortstops were small, quick men valued for their fielding skills. Many simply slapped at the ball when they were at the plate.

Ripken was different. He stood six foot four and was much bigger than most other shortstops. Although he wasn't a fast runner, he had quick reflexes and a strong arm. He fielded his position well and made up for his lack of speed by always being ready and making sure he was playing the hitter in the proper place. And he could hit, too, not only for average but also for power. Alex has said, "He was the only shortstop I knew of that hit third in the lineup," the spot where most teams put their best hitter.

In 1982, his first full season with the Orioles, Ripken was named American League Rookie of the Year. In 1983 he was named the league's Most Valuable Player.

As talented as Ripken was as a baseball player, he also possessed several more admirable qualities. He understood that he was a role model and worked hard to live up to his fans' expectations, signing autographs without complaint and always being polite. He never touted his own accomplishments and also possessed an extraordinary work ethic, one that would eventually help him to set the all-time record for consecutive games played.

Alex Rodriguez couldn't have selected a better ballplayer to emulate. He even kept a poster of Ripken over his bed.

He would lay on his bed gazing at the picture, and toss a baseball into the air over and over again, catching it on its way down. Every time he stepped on the baseball field, he imagined that he was Cal Ripken, and he tried to play the same way Ripken did. Like Ripken, Alex wanted to be a complete player and a good person.

His family was doing everything they could to make certain that Alex grew up in the right way. They made sure that he understood that school was more important than baseball. Alex loved learning and told his mother he might one day become a doctor or lawyer. His love of education made him different from other kids. He once admitted to a reporter, "I liked doing my homework."

His mother made sure that Alex knew how hard she had to work to support the family, so he would never take anything for granted. When she would return home from waitressing, Alex had to count her tip money, as much as forty or fifty dollars in bills and small change. It not only helped him with his math but also made him appreciate her efforts. She had to work for every single nickel and dime.

Like the Dominican Republic, Miami was warm all year round and enabled Alex to play baseball nearly every day. In addition to playing in the local youth leagues, Alex, J. D., and a group of other boys would spend much of their free time playing baseball. The boys would pitch to one another and take turns hitting until it was too dark to play.

Even then, Alex was one of the best players around. He was the only one on his team who could hit fast pitches. That meant something in the Miami area. The entire state of Florida is a hotbed of baseball talent, and the competition is particularly fierce in Tampa and Miami. Both cities have sent many players into professional baseball.

Alex was bigger, stronger, and faster than most kids his age. Due to his Dominican upbringing, he'd already played more baseball than most boys his age. When Alex played in organized leagues, Mr. Arteaga would tell the coaches how good he was and predict that one day Alex would play in the major leagues.

Although Alex loved baseball more than anything else, he occasionally found time for other sports. He played basketball and possessed a deadly shot and playmaking skills far beyond his years. And he played football, usually quarterback, where his strong arm translated into long touchdown passes.

Yet it was his skills on the baseball diamond that really made him stand out. When Alex was in junior high school, he played on several traveling teams for the best players in his age group. He played in tournaments all over Florida and the southeastern United States.

But as talented as he was, his coaches were even more impressed by his work habits and the way he carried himself. Tony Quesada, who coached one of Alex's traveling teams, later told a reporter that he was startled one morning in the team hotel to wake up at 7:00 A.M. and discover Alex already awake and doing his morning routine of 100 sit-ups and 100 push-ups.

As one of Alex's teammates recalled, on such trips "most guys would be in the hotel pool or goofing off. Alex would be in his room watching ESPN," studying the way major leaguers played.

As Alex prepared to enter high school in ninth grade, he and his family had a decision to make. Where would he attend school?

One option was to remain in public school. But

his mother worried about him. The local public high school was huge, and although most of the students were respectful and well behaved, some kids were in gangs, and other students just didn't care about learning. She worried that Alex's education might suffer in such an environment.

She was also concerned about the school's sports program. Alex had a special talent, and she wanted to make sure he received the proper instruction to take advantage of his skills.

The other option was a private school, Westminster Christian Academy. The school was much smaller than the local public school, with only about two hundred students in the high school program. Classes were small and there was more focus on academics than in many public schools. The school's religious curriculum was also attractive to Alex's mother. She wanted to make sure that Alex stayed on track and grew up to be a responsible, respectful young man. Teachers were strict at Westminster, and every student had to wear a school uniform.

Westminster also had a terrific sports program.

Even though the school was small, its teams were among the best in Florida. Playing sports at Westminster would expose Alex to highest level of competition in the state.

There was just one problem. The private school was not free. One year's tuition at the school cost nearly 7,000 dollars.

That was a lot of money to Alex's mother.

Chapter Three:

1990–1992

The Warrior

Lourdes Rodriguez had always dedicated her life to her children. The more she thought about Alex's future, the more she thought that Westminster was the best place for her son, not only for Alex the baseball player but Alex the person.

She had worked hard over the years and had opened her own immigration counseling office, which helped people from the Dominican Republic and other countries get settled in the United States and become legal residents and American citizens.

The high cost of the school didn't enter into her final decision. Once she decided that Alex should attend Westminster, she sat down and began to figure out how she would pay for it. She decided she would work a second job to enable her to pay the tuition. She took a part-time job as a waitress and started saving money. Eventually, she even opened her own restaurant.

She explained to Alex that she couldn't afford to send him to Westminster for ninth grade, but planned on sending him there the following year. In the meantime, Alex had to continue working hard at school and keep his grades up.

Alex knew his mother was making a big sacrifice. He promised to work hard and never let her down.

At the end of ninth grade, he applied to Westminster and was accepted. Now he knew he would have to work even harder.

At first Alex was a little intimidated at Westminster. The school was so small that everyone knew everyone else. The students came from all over Miami. Some were very wealthy and drove fancy new cars to school. And classes were much more difficult. There was a lot of homework, and Alex had to learn to budget his time to make sure he got everything done.

But he adjusted quickly to the school. He loved

learning and thrived in the classroom. He joined the football team and quickly made friends. Soon he was one of the most popular kids in his class. He had a quick smile and never acted like a big shot. And the girls at the school liked the handsome new boy with the green eyes.

Alex made friends with everyone, boys and girls, white, black, and Latino. They nicknamed him "Cheech," after a Latino comedian. "I was born in New York and grew up in Miami," he once said. "I'm proud to be an American and proud my parents are Dominican." As one acquaintance of Alex's remarked, "Alex identifies with both cultures."

Alex could hardly wait for baseball season to begin. But he was also a little afraid. Westminster was the best team in Miami and one of the best in the entire state of Florida — in fact, they were one of the best baseball teams in the country.

In 1990 the Westminster Warriors had won the state AA baseball championship and had finished tenth in *USA Today*'s national ranking of high school baseball teams. Many of the seniors on the 1990 team were now playing in the top-level college programs, and pitcher Ron Caridad had been drafted by the Minnesota Twins and was playing professional baseball. Still, there were thirteen players returning from the state championship team. Alex wasn't sure he'd even make the team, much less get to play. Coach Rich Hofman had a well-deserved reputation as one of the best — and most demanding — high school baseball coaches in the country. He set high standards for his players.

He had built the school's baseball program from scratch. When he began coaching there, the school didn't even have a field to play on. In his first few seasons, the team hardly won a game.

But Hofman hadn't quit. He helped raise money to build a field and went to clinics all over the state to learn the ins and outs of coaching. Westminster started winning, and once they did, the program started to attract the best baseball players in Miami. By the 1980s they were a powerhouse, so strong that they had to travel all over the state to find teams willing to play them.

Hofman had heard of Alex Rodriguez even before Alex had enrolled in the school. J. D. attended Westminster and had told Hofman that his friend Alex was the best player in the city. Mr. Arteaga told the coach the same thing. "You have to see [Alex] to believe him," he told Hofman.

Hofman didn't pay much attention at first. As he later told a reporter, "Coaches are always being told that kind of stuff." He figured that Alex was just another good player but nothing special.

Things were going well for Alex, but then tragedy struck. Near the end of football season, J. D.'s father suffered a heart attack and died while attending a football game in which Alex and J. D. were playing. As Alex said later, "Everything he gave to his son he gave to me. I still play in his honor."

In fact, Alex later credited Mr. Arteaga with helping him realize what he had to do to fulfill his potential. After his death, Alex recalls, "I started trying to lead by example and never missed a day of school and always did my homework."

When baseball practice started, Coach Hofman finally got his first good look at the sophomore player. As Hofman later recalled, "Alex wasn't Superman. He was a tall, thin, not very strong kid. But he did have real nice actions. That helped him defensively, but he was not yet a polished hitter."

Indeed, at first Alex didn't stand out at all. He wasn't close to being the best player on the team. In a preview story in the *Miami Herald* in February of 1991, Hofman barely mentioned Alex. He touted J. D. as a future pitching star. Alex was just another infield candidate.

As Hofman later said, Alex spent most of the season "adjusting to our high-intensity program." Playing baseball was serious business at Westminster, and Hofman made sure his players worked hard.

At first Alex didn't even make the starting lineup. At the beginning of the season Hofman divided the position between Alex and two other players. Eventually, however, Alex won the job with his glove. His hitting, recalled Hofman, still needed improvement. "He swung at a lot of bad pitches," remembered the coach later.

It probably helped Alex to play on such a good team. He wasn't expected to be the big star and was able to relax and just play. Although Westminster wasn't as dominant as they had been in 1990, the team was still one of the best in the state. They easily qualified for the state tournament.

In the district finals they faced Gulliver, their biggest rival. Only a month before, they had just managed to beat Gulliver, 2–1, in one of the closest games of the year. Everyone expected another close game.

But no one quite knew what to expect in the rematch. Due to a sore arm, J. D. hadn't pitched since the last Gulliver game. And Gulliver's senior pitcher Omar Fernandez was one of the best high school pitchers in the country. Westminster had been the only team to beat him.

Meanwhile, Alex Rodriguez had been improving every day. In the first inning, he came to bat with a runner on base.

Fernandez wasn't too worried about Rodriguez. He had gotten him out easily a month earlier.

But not this time. Fernandez challenged Rodriguez with a fastball, and the young shortstop reacted.

"Crack!" The ball rocketed off his bat toward left-center field then just kept going.

The ball soared over the fence in what the *Miami*

Herald described as "a two-run monster that rainbowed its way over the 375-foot sign in left-center." The home run put the Warriors ahead, 2–0.

The blast rocked Fernandez and gave Alex's teammates confidence. They scored another run in the first and three more in the second to take a commanding lead. J. D. shut Gulliver out, and Westminster rolled to a crushing 10–0 victory.

Two weeks later, the Warriors needed only one more win to make the state championship round. All they had to do was beat Clearwater Central Catholic.

Westminster went ahead in the first, scoring twice, including one run when the opposing pitcher tried to pick Alex off base and threw wildly. J. D. was able to score from third on the play.

Entering the fifth inning, Westminster led, 4–0. J. D. was throwing a no-hitter. Then everything went bad for Westminster.

J. D. lost his no-hitter when the first batter singled. Then the Westminster defense made several errors. Clearwater scored five runs and went on to win, 5–4.

Alex was disappointed, but he'd had a good season. He worked out extra hard in the off-season. He played quarterback on the football team, which he led to a 9–1 record. Collegiate football scouts touted him as one of the best quarterbacks in the state.

When the baseball team got together for their first practice of Alex's junior year, Coach Hofman could barely believe his eyes.

Alex had matured. He'd grown two inches taller and added thirty pounds of muscle. The gangly sophomore had turned into a prospect. Alex now stood six foot two and weighed 185 pounds. He hadn't lost any speed. In fact, he'd gotten faster and quicker. Most important, he was much stronger than the previous year.

Coach Hofman realized that Alex could be a special ballplayer. He began to spend more time with him, filling the role of surrogate father that Mr. Arteaga had once held. "I think he depended on me for advice," the coach later recalled. "We had sort of an adopted father/son relationship." Even today, Alex remains close to Coach Hofman, often working out at the school in the off-season and occasionally flying Hofman in to see him play.

Still, the Warriors were a deep and experienced team with a number of seniors who were considered stars. Although Alex was now one of the better players on the team, he still wasn't the big star.

But the opposition quickly took notice of his improved strength. By the end of the season, pitchers were afraid to throw the ball over the plate to him. His bat was so fast and powerful they hardly ever threw him a fastball. The only chance they had to get him out was to throw slower pitches, like change-ups and curveballs, and hope Alex would be overanxious and strike out.

Fat chance. Alex was becoming more and more disciplined at the plate and collecting more and more walks. With his speed, he could steal bases almost at will, so receiving a walk was almost like hitting a double.

Westminster roared through the regular season, losing only three times. They easily qualified for the state tournament and made it to the finals against Melbourne Florida Air Academy.

Alex got his team off to a good start. He batted leadoff and began the game with a tapper over the pitcher's head. The shortstop fielded the ball, but Alex streaked to first and beat his throw. The second hitter walked, then Doug Mientkiewicz, who now plays in the major leagues for the Minnesota Twins, moved Alex to third base with a ground ball. He scored when Westminster's clean-up hitter, Mickey Lopez, who also later played professionally, beat out an infield hit.

That's just about all the help J. D. needed. He slammed the door on Melbourne, shutting them out on five hits. Westminster won, to capture the state AA championship. A few weeks later, the team was named the number-one high school team in the country by USA Today. Alex was one of an incredible eight Westminster players to be named to the all-state team and along with teammate Steve Butler, a pitcher, he was named a high school All-American.

His statistics were mind-boggling. Despite being pitched around all year, Alex hit .477. In 35 games he stole an amazing 42 bases and scored 51 runs! He got on base with either a hit or a walk almost 60 percent of the time and cracked six home runs.

Already, Alex was hearing from college baseball coaches who were offering him scholarships. Baseball scouts began to whisper that if Alex Rodriguez wanted to play professionally, he'd be a top draft pick. With his senior year looming ahead, Alex knew he would soon have some decisions to make.

Chapter Four:
1992-1993

Superman?

In the summer of 1992, Alex's star only rose higher. He played on a United States national team against teams from all over, giving baseball scouts plenty of opportunities to see him play. Facing stiffer competition than in high school, Alex was even better than the scouts had thought.

It was becoming clear that Alex was the rarest kind of ballplayer, a player scouts call a "five-tool player." The phrase refers to the five skills baseball scouts look for in a player — the ability to run, throw, field, hit, and hit with power. Few players, even in the big leagues, have more than two or three of those skills in abundance. Players with all five skills are often stars like Willie Mays and Ken Griffey Jr.

Alex was hearing rumors that if he decided to go right into professional baseball, he might be one of the first players taken in the draft held each spring for amateur players. Being one of the first players selected could mean a contract with a signing bonus of more than one million dollars.

But at the same time, Alex was thinking about attending college. A college degree had always been one of his goals.

Alex had even decided which college he would attend if he didn't sign a professional baseball contract. He accepted a baseball scholarship to the University of Miami. He hoped to become a teacher one day. He knew that sometime in the next year he would have to decide whether to turn pro or to attend college. Until then, he was looking forward to playing his senior season in both football and baseball. He was even considering trying to play both sports in college.

Then something happened that changed everything. Hurricane Andrew hit the Miami area, knocking down buildings, causing flooding, and injuring hundreds of area residents. Although Alex and his family and friends were unhurt, the storm devastated the area and caused three million dollars' worth of damage to Westminster, including extensive damage to the baseball field.

The hurricane made Alex realize how quickly everything could change. He'd never before considered the possibility that he might be injured. Now he did.

That led him to make another decision. Despite being a star quarterback, Alex opted not to play football his senior year of high school. The threat of injury simply wasn't worth the risk to his baseball career. He decided to focus entirely on baseball. He knew that if he played to the best of his ability, at the end of the baseball season he would still have the option to either play professionally or go to college.

Throughout the fall all he did was study and work out. As he told a writer later, "I was the most boring guy in high school. I didn't go to the prom or homecoming. I was so focused on baseball."

At the beginning of the baseball season, the magazine *Baseball America*, which covers high school and collegiate baseball closely, named Alex the number-one high school prospect in the country. One respected college coach described him by saying, "If you were to sit in front of a computer and say, 'How would I construct the perfect shortstop?' you'd put all the data in, and then you would see Alex Rodriguez."

The pressure on Rodriguez was intense. *USA Today*'s preseason poll had already selected Westminster as the best team in the country. Everyone expected Westminster to win the state championship again. And they expected Alex to be the big star. Before the start of the season, Coach Hofman warned him that he would see a lot of scouts at their first game.

Alex nodded but was unconcerned. There were scouts at almost every game Westminster played. He was accustomed to their presence, and they had never affected his performance.

But when Alex took the field for the Warriors' first game, he was stunned.

Sixty-eight scouts, fully two-thirds of the crowd of about one hundred spectators, sat in the stands, notebooks, stopwatches, and radar guns in hand.

Every time he moved, they all took notes. Every time he ran to first base, he could hear their stopwatches click on and off. And every time he threw the ball, he could tell that they were aiming their radar guns to measure the speed of his throws.

Despite all the distractions, Alex played well in the opener. After the game, a reporter from out of town sought Alex out and started asking him questions.

"How did you find out about me?" asked Alex, puzzled. When the reporter explained that it was because he was considered the best baseball prospect in years, Alex could hardly believe it.

That night he spoke to his mother about all the attention he was suddenly receiving. It was starting to make him uncomfortable. He didn't know how to act.

His mother thought for a moment and then told her son, "The scouts are there because they have already seen something they like. So don't change. Just be yourself."

That was the best advice he could have received, because as the season continued, the attention on

Alex increased. At his next game, *seventy-two* scouts showed up. The opposition promoted his appearance as if he were a prizefighter or something. Crowds of more than a thousand fans became commonplace at Westminster games, an extraordinary number for a high school game. Kids mobbed him for his autograph. Before one road game, the local paper heralded Alex's appearance with a headline that read, SUPERMAN IS COMING TO TOWN! He found all the attention embarrassing.

He even contacted Derek Jeter, now a major league shortstop, who was then in his first year of minor league baseball, to ask his advice on how to handle all the attention. The year before, when he was in high school, Jeter had been just as highly touted as Rodriguez was now. Jeter told him to try to stay focused on the game. The two immediately hit it off and became good friends.

Alex didn't allow anything to affect his play. He just kept getting better. In the first ten games of the season, he hit .600 with seven home runs, 21 RBIs, and 12 steals. During one stretch, he reached base an incredible 21 times in a row! Westminster started the season 10–0.

Then they faced a tough Coral Gables team. The two teams played a night game and nearly 2,000 fans turned out to watch. Westminster pitcher Steve Butler, plagued by some poor defense, lost his first game in more than two years and Alex was held to only one hit and made a costly error. Westminster lost, 8–5.

But as the season continued, Alex somehow managed to stay on an even keel. Every time he came to bat, the opposing pitcher threw as if it were the last game of the World Series. Scouts told Coach Hofman that according to their radar guns, most pitchers threw three or four miles per hour faster to Alex than they did to other hitters.

Westminster cruised through the regular season and finished with only four losses. They entered the state tournament as heavy favorites to repeat as state AA champions.

Early in the tournament, they faced West Palm Beach Cardinal Newman. West Palm had a good team, but no one expected them to defeat Westminster.

But West Palm wasn't intimidated. They played cleanly and crisply, while Westminster was out of sync. Entering the sixth inning, Westminster trailed, 3–0.

Alex led off for Westminster in the sixth. He knew he had to get on base and start a rally. Coach Hofman flashed him the bunt sign.

Alex nodded. He knew West Palm wouldn't be expecting the greatest prospect in all of baseball to put down a bunt. The third baseman was playing deep.

As the pitcher wound up, Alex waited. At the very last second, as the pitcher's arm began to swing forward, Alex pivoted on his toes to face the pitcher and slid his top hand down the bat, holding it chest high and almost parallel to the ground.

Just as the pitcher released the ball, an infielder yelled out, "Bunt, bunt!" to alert his teammates. But by the time they heard him, Alex had already caught the ball on the fat part of the bat and directed it softly down the third-base line. Then he dropped his bat and started running as fast as he could.

He dashed toward first base. The surprised third baseman charged in and bent to pick up the slowly rolling ball. He scooped it up and threw as quickly as he could toward first.

Alex didn't see any of this. He just ran as hard as he could, arms and legs pumping in unison. As he neared the bag, he took one final long stride.

He saw the first baseman reach out, then pull his foot off the base. The ball, a white blur, went skipping past.

The throw was wild! Alex put on the brakes, turned, and raced toward second. By the time West Palm chased down the ball, he was standing safely on the bag!

The next player walked, bringing up Steve Butler. With two strikes, Coach Hofman put on the double steal. Alex and his teammate broke for the next bases as soon as the pitcher started his delivery.

Both players slid in safely. Butler struck out, but Westminster now had two runners in scoring position.

When the next hitter came to bat, Alex danced dangerously off third base. He distracted the pitcher and catcher, and a pitch bounced free. Alex trotted home to give Westminster their first run. A moment later, a teammate singled in the other runner to make the score 3–2.

It was still 3–2 at the beginning of the seventh and final inning. With one out, Warrior Robert Perez bunted for a hit. That brought up Alex.

The crowd was roaring. All his teammates were on their feet in the dugout. There was no other player Coach Hofman wanted at the plate.

The West Palm pitcher had to give Alex a pitch to hit. If he walked him, Perez would move into scoring position.

Alex stood in the batter's box and tried to relax. He focused all his attention on the pitcher.

The hurler wound up and threw. Alex uncoiled, and — *Pow!* — the ball exploded off his bat.

It rocketed over the left fielder's head on a low line, then cleared the fence and took a huge bounce. Home run! Westminster led, 4–3!

Alex started jogging around the bases as Perez dashed home, and the Warriors exploded from the bench, leaping with joy.

But as Alex rounded second base, the umpire motioned for him to stop. "The ball bounced over the fence," he said. "It's a ground-rule double." Alex stopped, and his mouth hung open in disbelief. He knew he had hit a home run. But he didn't argue. He just stood on second base.

Coach Hofman ran out on the field and briefly argued with the umpire, but it did no good. Although the umpire was the only person on the field who didn't see the ball go over the fence, his opinion was the only one that mattered. The score was tied, 3–3, and Alex was on second.

A moment later, it seemed not to matter when Steve Butler singled, scoring Alex and putting Westminster ahead. But West Palm tied the game in the bottom of the seventh to force the game into extra innings.

The score remained knotted until the last of the ninth. With a West Palm runner on second base, the batter hit a routine ground ball to Alex at shortstop.

Alex had made similar plays a thousand times. He shuffled his feet quickly to get in front of the ball and kept his hands low, his glove touching the ground. As the ball bounced toward him he scooped it up, transferred it from his glove to his hand, pivoted, and threw to first base, making his usual strong throw.

But this time, something went wrong. His throw was too strong. The ball went wide.

The runner on second took off and rounded third as the ball skipped away down the right-field line. As several Westminster players scrambled after it, the West Palm team raced from their bench and surrounded home plate. The runner scored without a throw, then disappeared into the throng. West Palm won, 5–4.

Alex Rodriguez stood at shortstop, a blank look on his face. On the last play of his high school career, on a play he had made a thousand times, he had made an error, and his team had lost.

It was over.

Chapter Five:
1993

A Long Summer

Coach Hofman was philosophical after the game. "Those plays he does with his eyes closed," he said. "He's meant so much to this team. He's done so much. You can't fault him. He's human."

Everyone understood. Errors are a part of baseball. Alex knew that even his hero, Cal Ripken, sometimes made errors.

Alex finished the year with a .505 batting average, nine home runs, 38 RBIs, and 38 stolen bases. He walked 30 times and reached base 89 times in 129 plate appearances for an incredible on-base percentage of .712. Nothing he had done all year had made the baseball scouts think less of him. In fact, some were predicting that he would be the first player selected in the draft, scheduled to take place on June 3.

In his three-year career at Westminster, Alex had hit a robust .419, scored 135 runs, knocked in 70, and cracked 17 home runs. Although he'd made 24 errors, he'd also stolen 90 bases in 94 tries.

Alex was looking forward to draft day. He knew that it would determine his future. If he was offered enough money, he planned on signing a professional contract. He wanted to take care of his mother. But if he wasn't offered a large enough contract, he planned on going to the University of Miami, where he would be eligible for the draft again after his junior year.

With the help of some family friends, Alex and his mother had already selected an agent to help him with his negotiations with professional baseball. They selected Scott Boras, an agent known as a tough negotiator.

In the weeks before the draft, Alex tried to enjoy his final days of high school and graduation. All year long, school and the baseball field were the only two places he had felt comfortable and relaxed. But at the same time, he had enjoyed every minute. "Someone asked me if I felt relieved because [high school] is over," he said at the time. "No, I would like to start all over and do it again."

Most observers expected Alex to be either the first pick, held by the Seattle Mariners, or the second pick, held by the Los Angeles Dodgers. The other big prospect was college pitcher Darren Dreifort. Dreifort was older and considered less risky and closer to being ready for the big leagues than Alex. If the Mariners decided to choose Dreifort, the Dodgers would probably select Alex with the second pick.

Alex hoped to be picked by the Dodgers. He wanted to play outside in warm weather, and in the National League, so his family could see him play in person whenever the Dodgers traveled to play the Florida Marlins in Miami.

In Seattle, the weather was often cool and damp. The Mariners played in a dome that wasn't very attractive, and as an American League team, they never traveled to Florida. A week before the draft, he even contacted the Mariners and asked them not to draft him. But the team remained convinced that if they did decide to draft him, they could convince Rodriguez to sign.

The night before the draft, Alex and his closest friends took a harbor cruise together to celebrate the end of the school year and the beginning of the next stage of their lives.

On the day of the draft, Alex, his family and friends, and members of the press gathered at Alex's second home, his friend J. D.'s house, for a draft day party. Nearly one hundred people gathered in the back-yard and on the patio to await a phone call from the team that drafted Alex.

Meanwhile, at draft headquarters, several mem-bers of the Seattle Mariners front office huddled to-gether, trying to decide whom to draft. The Mariners already had one great young hitter, Ken Griffey Jr. They needed pitching, and some team officials wanted the club to draft Dreifort.

But Seattle's scouting reports touted Rodriguez as a "once in a lifetime" kind of player. When *Baseball America* had reported that the Mariners were more likely to pick Dreifort than Rodriguez, their Miami-area scout, Fernando Arguelles, had cried. But as team vice president of scouting and development Roger Jongewaard explained later, "We decided to roll the dice and go with the position player."

At 1:14 P.M. the telephone rang at J. D.'s house. The Mariners were on the line. They had selected Alex! If they could agree on a contract, Alex would join the Mariners organization.

Alex was a little disappointed that the Dodgers hadn't drafted him, but he was still excited. "Yeah, I'm glad I'm number one," Alex told the press moments later. "I'm number one and have to live up to that. It's like starting a new chapter. I was pretty confident Seattle would take me."

Then a reporter asked Alex if he thought he would sign with the Mariners or eventually decide to take his scholarship to the University of Miami.

"I'm not in a rush," Alex explained. "It depends on how nice [the Mariners] want to be in negotiations. We just want something that is fair." His sister, Susy, then added, "Hopefully they will be fair. My brother is one of the most wholesome players anywhere. We just want to be treated fair."

Everyone was happy. Susy started crying, and

everyone congratulated Alex. Then, an hour later, it was Alex's turn to offer the congratulations. Teammate Dan Perkins, a pitcher, was selected by the Minnesota Twins in the second round.

"I owe a lot to Alex," Perkins said. "The scouts came to see him, and I guess they thought I wasn't too bad, either."

Coach Hofman talked to the press about both players. Of Alex he said, "He has three tools he could use in the majors right now. He has speed, he has arm strength, and he has defense. The only question that remains is if he can hit [major league pitching]." Then he added, "I hope they allow him to progress at a natural rate."

Later that day, the phone rang again. Someone answered it, and the caller asked for Alex. Alex expected it to be one of his friends or perhaps another reporter.

But when Alex heard the voice on the other end of the line, he was stunned.

It was his father!

He couldn't believe it. For years, Alex had hoped

that he would someday hear from his father again, but now that it was happening, he wasn't sure how he felt. After all the years his father had been away, "I didn't know what to think," Alex later recalled.

His father congratulated him, and they chatted awkwardly for a few minutes. Then his father said good-bye. The call had brought back some painful memories. Alex didn't know if he would ever speak to his father again. He wasn't even certain he was happy he had called in the first place.

A few weeks later, Alex was named *USA Today's* national high school player of the year. His agent and the Mariners soon began negotiating.

Alex hoped the two sides could come to a quick agreement. He was eager to begin his professional career.

But it soon became obvious that the Mariners and Rodriguez were far apart. His agent, Scott Boras, believed Alex deserved the largest contract any high school draft pick had ever received, more than one million dollars. The Mariners didn't want to pay that much.

Neither side would budge, and their meetings became contentious. Boras soon insisted that the Mariners communicate only through faxes.

Alex just wanted to play, but he didn't want to be taken advantage of, either. Unless the Mariners met his demands, he said, he planned on taking the athletic scholarship to the University of Miami.

Sports writers from all over the country started writing about Alex's contract negotiations. Very few of them took his side. They thought he had no right to demand so much money before he had ever even played a professional game. They called him "selfish" and "arrogant." Alex cringed every time he read another story about himself in the paper.

All he wanted to do was play baseball, but until he signed a contract, he wasn't allowed to play for one of the Mariner farm clubs. But he could still play amateur baseball.

But even that became problematic. Alex was invited to try out for Team USA's senior squad, the team that provides many of the members of the U.S. Olympic team. Alex hoped to play in the Olympics.

But one of the sponsors of the team, a baseball card company, planned to make a set of baseball cards with all the players' images. The company didn't want to pay the players anything.

Alex's agent turned down Team USA's proposal. He knew that the first baseball card with Alex on it might someday be worth a whole lot of money. He didn't think it was fair for Alex to sign away his rights. When the company wouldn't back down, Alex was prevented from trying out.

He was crushed, but he still found an opportunity to play. Every year, the United States Olympic Committee holds an Olympic Festival to prepare young athletes for international competition. In baseball, teams are created that represent various regions of the country. They then play each other in a tournament as part of the Festival.

Alex joined the South team and traveled to the tournament in San Antonio, Texas. He was just happy to be playing baseball again.

But at the end of July, just a few days after Alex's eighteenth birthday, his career nearly ended before it even started. In one tournament game, as Alex sat on the bench, an errant throw flew into the dugout. Alex never saw it coming, and it hit the side of his face.

He immediately fell to the bench, holding his head. His teammates and coaches surrounded him. After a few scary moments, he was able to stand and was taken to the hospital.

Alex was very lucky. Although the ball had broken his cheekbone, his eye wasn't damaged. He would be sore and swollen for a few weeks, but the ball had not done lasting damage.

Both Alex and the Mariners breathed a sigh of relief. Then they started negotiating again.

But time was running out. Once Alex started attending classes at the University of Miami, the Mariners' rights to sign him would expire. The school year was nearly ready to begin, but Alex held off from enrolling in class, hoping the two sides would eventually come together.

Finally, just hours before his first class was scheduled to start, the Mariners and Alex's agent reached an agreement. The Mariners agreed to pay him a record-setting 1.3 million dollars. At the kitchen table of his mother's home, with his family and agent at his side along with several members of the Mariners front office, including team president Chuck Armstrong, Alex calmly and confidently signed his name to the contract. As his mother wiped tears from her face, Alex flashed a tired smile.

He was a professional baseball player. At last.

Chapter Six:

1993

Minor Leaguer for a Minute

Alex found the amount of his contract mind-boggling. But he didn't lose perspective over what was important.

Immediately after signing the contract, he asked to speak to club president Chuck Armstrong in private. The first thing he did was apologize for any hard feelings that might have developed during the tough negotiations. That was just business. He assured Armstrong that he was happy to be a Mariner and planned on doing his very best.

A lot of young men who had just signed a contract like Alex's might have let the money go to their head, but that wasn't Alex's way. With the help of his agent, his family set up an investment plan and put

Alex on a strict budget. Every month, he would receive $500 in cash and a $500 allowance on a credit card. Alex didn't know it at the time, but that was even less than the minimum minor league salary!

He made only one special purchase. He was allowed to buy a new car, a black-and-gold Jeep. He also planned to buy his mother a nice present for her birthday. He knew that without her support, he never would have turned into the player, or the person, that he had become.

He was able to give her the greatest present of all. Alex's big contract allowed his mother to retire. He paid off the mortgage of her house and bought her a brand-new Mercedes-Benz. "My mom is the whole story of my life," he once said. "She's my whole inspiration. She deserves everything. She's done so much for me."

That's what made Alex's mother most proud. She didn't care if he got a hit or not, but when she saw how he behaved, or someone told her that her son was polite and respectful, she beamed with pride.

Had Rodriguez signed with the Mariners earlier that summer, that team would have sent him to one of their minor league teams. But by the time Alex signed, the minor league season was just about over.

Fortunately, in October the major leagues sponsor what are known as "instructional leagues." In an instructional league, veteran players practice new skills or try to fine-tune their talent, while younger players gain valuable experience in a relaxed setting. They practice every morning and play games in the afternoon. The final score doesn't matter. Everybody is just trying to improve.

The Mariners sent Alex to play in the instructional league in Peoria, Arizona. It gave the Mariners a chance to teach Alex how to play professional baseball and assess his progress.

John McNamara, who'd been in professional baseball for forty-five years, managed the team. He'd been a big league manager for Cincinnati, Boston, and California.

He'd heard about Rodriguez but had never seen him play. He didn't expect much. Even the most highly touted prospect is usually light years away from being good enough to play in the major leagues at such a young age.

But Alex made an immediate impression on his manager. In his first game, he denied five batters hits with his great fielding.

"You couldn't ask for a better-played game of shortstop," McNamara later said. "The kid looks and plays mature. He's loaded with talent, all the tools they've been talking about."

Alex spent hours working with hitting coach Tommy Cruz, refining his swing. As Cruz explained it, Alex wasn't doing anything wrong, but he had to "get used to the hard stuff again." In high school, he simply hadn't seen too many fastballs. Pitchers had been afraid to throw them.

Rodriguez also had to learn to hit with a new kind of bat. High school players use aluminum bats. But in pro baseball, players must use wood bats. They have a much smaller "sweet spot," the best place for the bat to hit the ball, than aluminum bats and are much less forgiving. Many players have a hard time making an adjustment, but Rodriguez adapted quickly.

Rodriguez impressed the Mariners even more with the way he related to his teammates. Despite being the number one pick and an instant millionaire, Alex didn't have an attitude. He fit in and was well liked by his teammates. "He's a down to earth guy," said teammate Andy Sheets. "He works his butt off just like everybody else." When a sporting goods company sent Alex a huge supply of equipment, he gave most of it to his teammates. "The guys needed them, and I had plenty," he explained.

When the instructional league ended, Alex returned home for a few months and waited to see where the Mariners would send him to begin his minor league career. Already, some of the coaches and scouts in the organization were saying he was close to the big leagues. As a matter of fact, according to his contract, the Mariners would have to bring him up to the majors in September of 1994. They didn't have to play him, but they would have to call him up. Alex wanted to perform well enough so he would get an opportunity to play.

In late February, Alex traveled to the Mariners'

Alex Rodriguez, top draft pick of 1993, listens as the Seattle Mariners tell him the good news.

The newest and youngest member of the Seattle Mariners signs autographs after batting practice in 1994.

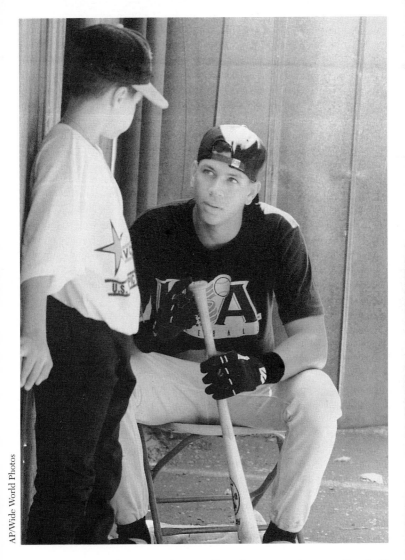

Alex Rodriguez takes time out to talk with a Major League Baseball hopeful.

Nimble moves like this one make A-Rod one of the best shortstops in baseball.

A-Rod cracks his first grand-slam homer in a game against the Detroit Tigers in 1996.

Even when it means flattening the opposition, Rodriguez makes the double play.

A-Rod slams a home run in game one of the American League Championship Series against the Yankees in 2000.

Two of the best shortstops in the league today: Alex Rodriguez and Derek Jeter square off during the second game of the 2000 A.L. Championship Series.

In a controversial play in game six of the 2004 ALCS, Alex Rodriguez slaps the ball out of Bronson Arroyo's glove. A-Rod was first called safe, but the call was reversed when the play was deemed illegal.

Alex Rodriguez is having a spectacular second season with the Yankees in 2005.

Alex Rodriguez's Career Statistics

Year	Team	AVG	G	AB	R	H	2B	3B	HR	RBI	BB	K	OBP	SLG
1994	SEA	.204	17	54	4	11	0	0	0	2	3	20	.241	.204
1995	SEA	.232	48	142	15	33	6	2	5	19	6	42	.264	.408
1996	SEA	.358	146	601	141	215	54	1	36	123	59	104	.414	.631
1997	SEA	.300	141	587	100	176	40	3	23	84	41	99	.350	.496
1998	SEA	.310	161	686	123	213	35	5	42	124	45	121	.360	.560
1999	SEA	.285	129	502	110	143	25	0	42	111	56	109	.357	.586
2000	SEA	.316	148	554	134	175	34	2	41	132	100	121	.420	.606
2001	TEX	.318	162	632	133	201	34	1	52	135	75	131	.399	.622
2002	TEX	.300	162	624	125	187	27	2	57	142	87	122	.392	.623
2003	TEX	.298	161	607	124	181	30	6	47	118	87	126	.396	.600
2004	NYY	.286	155	601	112	172	24	2	36	106	80	131	.375	.512
2005	NYY	.320	145	544	109	174	26	1	42	114	81	119	.420	.603
Totals		.307	1575	6134	1230	1881	335	25	423	1210	720	1245	.385	.576

Alex Rodriguez's Career Highlights

1993:
First overall draft pick

1996:
Named Associated Press Player of the Year
Member of the A.L. All-Star team
Finished second in voting for American League MVP
First shortstop to win batting title since 1944
Made Major League history with the most hits and extra-base
    hits and highest batting average by a shortstop

Led the league in batting average, with the highest in Major League
history by a player under 22
Won the A.L. Silver Slugger Award

1997:
Replaced veteran shortstop Cal Ripken as starting A.L. shortstop
in All-Star game
Third Mariner to ever post a 20/20 season (home runs and stolen bases)

1998:
Member of the A.L. All-Star team
Wrote the book *Hit a Grand Slam*
Third player, and first non-outfielder, in Major League history to post
a 40/40 season (home runs and stolen bases)

1999:
Member of the A.L. All-Star team
Posted his second consecutive 40 home run season, a first for a
shortstop

2000:
Selected Major League Player of the Year by *Baseball America*
Had most RBIs by a shortstop since 1959
Won the A.L. Silver Slugger Award

2001:
Member of the A.L. All-Star team

2002:
Member of the A.L. All-Star team
Winner of the American League Golden Glove Award

2003:
Winner of the American League Golden Glove Award
Named American League Most Valuable Player

2004:
Member of the A.L. All-Star team

2005:
Member of the A.L. All-Star team

spring training facility in Arizona. After only a few days working out with the major league team, he was assigned to the minor league camp. Still, Mariner manager Lou Piniella had been impressed with what he'd seen. He told the press that once Rodriguez made it to the major leagues, he expected him to stay.

At the end of camp, Rodriguez was assigned to the Mariners' single-A team, the Appleton (Wisconsin) Foxes of the Midwest League. The minor leagues are divided into several classifications. Rookie League is the lowest, followed by single-A, double-A, and triple-A. The Mariners were confident that Alex was good enough to skip Rookie League and go straight to A ball.

Minor league life was quite an adjustment for young Rodriguez. In the instructional league and at training camp, he'd stayed in a dormitory with the other players. But in Appleton, his living arrangements were up to him. Now that he was being paid like an adult, he was expected to live and act like one.

Alex moved into an apartment, which he shared

with teammate Alex Sutherland and his wife. He didn't want to be by himself, and he liked rooming with a married player. Already, strange girls were approaching him, attracted to his money as much as his good looks. And some minor leaguers, out on their own for the first time, spend much of their free time partying. Alex wasn't interested in those things. He was focused on playing baseball. Living with a married couple helped keep his distractions to a minimum.

But that wasn't the only adjustment Alex had to make. The fields in most Midwest League cities were awful, much worse than the one Alex had played on at Westminster. It was a long bus ride between each city, and Alex had to become accustomed to playing every day. Many minor leaguers, even those picked the first round, never make a successful adjustment to minor league life or reach their full potential. Alex was determined to succeed.

It didn't take long for him to learn an important lesson. The game of professional baseball was a very different game from the one he had grown up playing.

In the first week of the season, he cracked his first professional home run against the Springfield Sultans. It was a towering shot, one of the longest balls Alex had ever hit at the time, traveling some 440 feet.

Right after he swung, Alex knew he had hit the ball well. He savored the moment and stood at the plate admiring the hit. Then he flipped his bat away and slowly jogged around the bases.

The manager of the other team was furious. He charged Rodriguez with showing up his pitcher. Rodriguez didn't know it, but watching a home run and jogging slowly around the bases is considered to be poor sportsmanship in pro baseball.

Rodriguez was puzzled. When he got to the bench, his own manager, Carlos Lezcano, said nothing. Alex wasn't yet sure if he'd done anything wrong or not.

The next day, he quickly found out. In his first at bat, the Sultans' pitcher purposely hit him in the ribs with his first pitch. The umpire ejected the pitcher, but the pitcher's teammates and even his manager congratulated him when he walked off the mound.

Rodriguez jogged to first base. He asked the first base coach, "Was that on purpose?"

"It sure was," the coach snapped. The ball in his ribs was in retaliation for the way Rodriguez had behaved after the home run. Rodriguez understood that he had just been taught a valuable lesson.

Now manager Lezcano talked to him about the incident. He told Rodriguez that because of his big contract, everyone was going to be watching him closely. The opposition would always be gunning for him. He had to make extra sure that he didn't give the fans or the opposition the impression that he thought he was better than everyone else. He had to respect the game.

Alex learned quickly. Lezcano commented on it a few weeks later. "Now when he hits a home run," he said, laughing, "he's almost sprinting. I have to slow him down."

Still, Rodriguez got off to a relatively slow start. Over the first few weeks of the season, his batting average was a mere .280, and he had hit only one home run. Most players would have been delighted to hit .280, but Rodriguez expected more of himself. He began to doubt his own abilities.

He was frustrated. "I called my mother," he admitted later, "and told her 'I want to come home.'"

Lourdes Rodriguez knew just what to say. "I don't want you home with that attitude," she said. "You go out and play hard."

Rodriguez took her advice. Within a few weeks, he'd lifted his average above .300 and hit a few home runs. He called his mother again.

"That's better," she said. "Now you can call me, even collect."

The only other trouble Rodriguez had was being on time. He was supposed to be at the ballpark by 3:30 P.M. every day for mandatory stretching and pregame practice. Rodriguez cut it close, often jogging out to the field precisely at 3:30, still tucking in his uniform shirt. Lezcano, who was in regular contact with Alex's mother to keep her from worrying, mentioned the problem to her one day.

Once again, Rodriguez's mother knew just what to say to her son. The next day, recalled Lezcano later,

"He was there at 2:30 P.M., an hour before we stretched."

Soon it was Alex Rodriguez who was giving the lessons, teaching the opposition that he was a very special player. They learned that he could hit almost any pitch, and that he scooped up ground balls with the efficiency of a vacuum cleaner. They also learned that he could steal a base whenever he wished. Over a two-week period in early May, he hit .455, going 20 of 44 with an incredible 10 home runs. He was stubborn, too, continuing to play even after breaking his nose.

His teammates were amazed. "He's done things [on the field] I've never seen before," said one. "He's like a league above everybody else," said another.

The Mariners planned to allow Rodriguez to develop at his own pace. Many prospects who advance too quickly through the minor leagues suddenly find themselves over their heads. They become frustrated, lose confidence, and never reach their full potential. "This is not the year to rush him," said former major leaguer Jim Beattie, the Mariners' player-development director. "We're happy with him at Appleton. We're not going to help him by rushing him."

But Rodriguez's stellar play soon forced their hand. After only a few months in Appleton, the Mariners began to worry that by not moving him up, they were holding him back. Single-A baseball was just too easy for Rodriguez. Even though he was one of the youngest players in the league, he played like a man among boys. In only 65 games, he had already hit 15 home runs and knocked in 55. His batting average was well above .300.

So in mid-season, they sent him up a classification, to their double-A team in the Southern League in Jacksonville, Florida. In double-A baseball, most players already have three or four years of minor league experience and are twenty-two or twenty-three years old. Most players are considered prospects with a good chance of making the major leagues.

For many young professional players, the leap from single-A to double-A baseball is enormous. Every pitcher has two or three pitches they can throw for strikes. Players who were stars in single-A baseball often take a year or two to adjust to double-A, if they ever adjust at all.

But Rodriguez was special. In his very first double-A at bat, he cracked a home run. Double-A pitchers found him just as hard to get out as those in single-A had. And Rodriguez continued to field and run and throw like a major leaguer.

The Mariners were surprised. They knew Rodriguez was good, and they expected him to succeed, but they were stunned by his rate of progress. Alex didn't know it, but in Seattle there was someone who thought he was ready to take the next step.

Chapter Seven
1994

The Mariner

Since joining the American League as an expansion team in 1977, the Seattle Mariners had served as the doormat of the West division. Although the team had developed some fine players and occasionally flirted with a .500 season, they usually had to struggle to stay out of last place.

But under new manager Lou Piniella, who took over in 1993, there was reason for optimism in Seattle. Piniella had enjoyed a long career in the majors and had been a valuable outfielder for the world champion New York Yankees in 1977 and 1978. After retiring, he'd managed both the Yankees and the Cincinnati Reds, winning a World Series with the Reds in 1990. The fiery manager had a well-deserved reputation as an astute judge of talent, and he had demonstrated the ability to get the most out of his players.

That had been the case in Seattle in 1993. With a core of talented young stars like pitcher Randy Johnson, first baseman Tino Martinez, and outfielders Jay Buhner and Ken Griffey Jr., the Mariners had stunned the baseball world, challenging for the West division title before finishing in fourth place, only twelve games out of first. In 1994, everyone expected the Mariners to improve. Some people expected them to win the division title.

But in the first half of the 1994 season, very little had gone right for the Mariners. Apart from Randy Johnson, their pitching collapsed. Although the Mariners were hitting the ball as well as any team in the league, they found it hard to win and were struggling to reach .500.

In most seasons, they would have already been looking ahead to next year, but in 1994, every team in the West division was struggling. Despite their poor performance, the Mariners were only a few games out of first place and still had a chance to win the division.

Manager Piniella knew that the team had to do everything they could to try to make the playoffs. Every day, he received reports on every minor leaguer in the Mariners system, and every day he saw how well Rodriguez was playing.

When he had seen Rodriguez play during spring training, he believed that he could already play shortstop at the major league level. His maturity and the way he behaved had also impressed Piniella, who later said, "You get vibes from young players. The kid who is scared sits at the end of the bench. This spring, when I was ready to make my substitutions, Alex always became highly visible. He would grab a bat or his glove. In his own way, he was telling me he was ready." Now, based upon Rodriguez's minor league performance, Piniella believed he was ready to face big league pitching.

The Mariners needed a spark, and Piniella thought Alex Rodriguez could supply it. Current shortstop Felix Fermin was hitting .300, and although he was a good fielder, he didn't have much range for a shortstop. And second base had been a problem for the team all year. Piniella had tried several players at the position without success. Those who could hit couldn't field, and those who fielded well couldn't hit. Piniella wanted to bring Rodriguez to the big leagues to play shortstop and move Fermin to second base.

The Mariners front office resisted the move. Although Ken Griffey Jr. had made the leap to the major leagues at age nineteen, he was considered a rarity. Very few players are ready to play in the major leagues at such a young age. Griffey had the advantage of growing up in a baseball family. His father, Ken Sr., had been a big leaguer. Ken Griffey Jr. hadn't been intimidated by the major leagues.

And he had been nineteen. Rodriguez was still eighteen. In the previous twenty years or so, only a handful of eighteen-year-olds had played in the major. Most hadn't been successful, at least not right away.

Piniella spent several days arguing with the Mariners front office over his request to bring Rodriguez to the major leagues. Even Rodriguez's manager in Jacksonville told the front office he didn't believe the shortstop was ready.

But Piniella wouldn't give in. The front office reluctantly agreed to bring Rodriguez to the major leagues.

His manager gave him the news in Jacksonville on July 6, 1994. The next day, he would fly to Boston and meet the Mariners, who were playing the Red Sox.

Rodriguez couldn't believe it. He was happy, but also afraid. Only fourteen months before, he had been playing high school baseball. Now, he was going to the major leagues.

He called home and spoke to his sister first, giving her the good news. At the end of their conversation, he asked her to pray for him. When his Jacksonville teammates found out that Rodriguez had been called up, they were happy for him, but Rodriguez was still uncertain. He told them he thought the Mariners were "crazy."

Then he got excited. He started calling all his friends and told them the news. He made sure he called Coach Hofman, too. Everyone told Rodriguez they had confidence in him and they thought that he would do fine.

Later that day, his mother flew from Miami to Jacksonville to see him off. When she arrived in Jacksonville, she helped her son pack. Mother and son spent most of the night talking. Alex was so excited, he barely slept. Mrs. Rodriguez didn't sleep at all.

The next day, at 6 A.M., she drove her son to the airport to catch his flight. He carried his bags into the airport, and when his flight was called, he stood before his mother. He gave her a big hug and whispered, "I love you so much."

His mother tried not cry. As she said later, "I am his mother and his father. I wanted to cry, but I couldn't show him that I was worried or scared. I am the tree trunk of the family. The trunk cannot fall or else the branches fall with it."

She told her son good-bye and watched as he walked away and boarded the plane. Then she cried. A few hours later, she followed her son to Boston. She had to see his first game.

When Alex got to Boston, he took a cab and met the team at the hotel, then accompanied them to Fenway Park later that afternoon. As he walked into the old ballpark, he could hardly believe where he was. Some of the game's greatest players, like Red Sox stars Babe Ruth and Ted Williams, had started their major league careers in Fenway Park. And now, it was Alex Rodriguez's turn.

He met some of his teammates and endured some good-natured teasing about his age. Manager Lou Piniella didn't waste any time. When Rodriguez entered the visiting club's locker room, he saw that Piniella had penciled him into the starting lineup.

Ken Griffey Jr. was the first Mariner player to greet him in the clubhouse. He motioned Rodriguez to the locker right next to his. He knew exactly how Rodriguez felt. Five years earlier, when he was nineteen, he had been in the same shoes.

That didn't prevent him from teasing his young teammate, though. He handed him some coupons to a fast food restaurant. "You're making one point three million," he quipped. "When you get sent back down to the minors, take the guys out to lunch down there." Then he smiled.

A few minutes later, one of his teammates, veteran relief pitcher Rich Gossage, known as "the

Goose," approached Rodriguez and introduced himself. The two chatted for a few moments, and Rodriguez mentioned that he had played in Appleton, Wisconsin, earlier that year.

Gossage nodded and said, "I played in Appleton, too."

Alex perked up. "Yeah?" he said excitedly. "When was that? Nineteen eighty-eight?"

Gossage looked at Rodriguez for a moment, and a smile slowly broke out on his face.

"Uh, no," he said. "Nineteen seventy-one."

Rodriguez's eyes opened wide and his jaw dropped open.

"Wow," he said, "I was born in *nineteen seventy-five.*"

Gossage, in fact, had just turned forty-three years old. He had been in the major leagues since 1972, three years before Rodriguez had been born!

Before the game, manager Piniella met with the local press. They asked him whether Rodriguez was ready.

Piniella took responsibility for the move. "If it doesn't work out, I'm the one who's going to be criticized. This team has struggled, so why not let him play?" he said. "We were going to call him up next year anyway, and six or seven weeks of double-A ball was not going to make a huge difference."

Rodriguez was growing more confident by the minute. "I know I'm ready," he said.

Fenway Park was packed for the Friday night game. Despite his confidence, when Rodriguez took his place at shortstop before the game, his stomach was full of butterflies. He had never played baseball before so many people in his life. As he said later, "It's funny, but last year I would have paid anything to watch a major league game. This year I'm playing in one."

Then Goose Gossage sauntered by on his way to the bullpen. He caught Rodriguez's eye and said, "You nervous, kid?"

As Rodriguez stammered to respond, the grizzled old pitcher gave him a big wink and smiled. Knowing that Gossage felt he belonged made Rodriguez feel a lot better.

Rodriguez's first game proved memorable. The first few innings went by in a rush, as he went hitless in his first two at bats and didn't have a ball hit to him. But in the fifth inning, he finally got his feet wet, fielding a routine ground ball and flipping it to Fermin for a force out at second base.

Then Boston's Tim Naehring came up. He smashed a hard ground ball to the left side.

Rodriguez reacted. He glided far to his right, into what is known as the "hole" between the shortstop and third baseman, backhanded the ground ball, set himself, and made the long throw across the diamond.

"Out!" called the umpire. His throw beat the runner by a half step and earned him a nice round of applause from the crowd. Even veteran shortstops sometimes have trouble with the play, but Rodriguez had been flawless.

The next inning, Rodriguez witnessed a play that had happened only nine times in baseball history. With no outs and runners on first and second, Seattle batter Marc Newfield hit a line drive up the middle. Boston shortstop John Valentin stabbed the ball in the air, stepped on second to double off the runner, then tagged the runner from first going to second.

The second base umpire pumped his arm three times. "Out! Out! Out!" he called.

The crowd was stunned, then started cheering. The inning was over. Valentin had made an unassisted triple play, the rarest play in baseball!

Seattle lost, 4–3, but Rodriguez had had a great time. "It was a great game!" he said. "Except that we lost. I had fun."

But no one was more excited than Rodriguez's mother. "It was incredible," she said later. "I kept asking myself, 'Am I dreaming?'" Her son was a major leaguer at last.

Rodriguez was more relaxed in his second game. He made another great fielding play, but came up to bat in the fourth inning still looking for his first major league hit.

Pitcher Sergio Valdez jammed him, but Rodriguez still managed to get the bat on the ball and ground the pitch toward the hole. Third baseman Scott Cooper reached out and fielded the ball, then gathered himself and threw to first. Most major leaguers would have been out.

But Rodriguez wasn't like most major leaguers. He ran as hard as his legs could carry him and dashed across the bag just ahead of the throw.

"Safe!" It was a hit! Following baseball tradition, the Boston first baseman flipped the ball to the Seattle first-base coach so Rodriguez could have a souvenir of his first major league hit.

On the next pitch, the Mariners' third-base coach gave Rodriguez the steal sign. He watched the pitcher closely, and as soon as he began to throw home, Rodriguez took off.

He slid into second base. "Safe!" A stolen base!

In the eighth inning, Rodriguez came to bat again against Scott Bankhead. This time, he ripped the ball through the hole for a clean hit. Seattle went on to win, 7–4. Rodriguez was on his way.

Of course, he didn't play great every day. No major leaguer does. The next day, he struck out three times and made an error. But Rodriguez took it in stride. "Every young player has days like that," he said. "I'm a typical young player. Hopefully, there won't be too many that rough."

While it was clear that he was still learning, he wasn't overmatched or intimidated by being in the big leagues. The Mariners were pleased with his progress. He was fielding well, and although he wasn't hitting with power, he was having good at bats and getting some hits.

But all season long, a dark cloud had hovered over big league baseball. In August, it burst. The contract between the players and owners had expired, and the two sides had been unable to reach a new agreement. The owners, in an attempt to force an agreement, announced plans to shut down the season on August 11. Any player on the major league roster at that time would be unable to keep playing, even in the minor leagues, until an agreement was reached.

The Mariners didn't want a young player like Rodriguez to have to sit out. He needed to keep playing. They knew that all he needed to be a star was experience.

So on August 2, just before the season was shut

down, the Mariners sent Rodriguez back to the minor leagues, this time to their triple-A team in Calgary, Alberta, Canada. He was disappointed, but understood. He didn't want to sit out, either. He wanted to play ball.

Eventually, the remainder of the major league season, including the World Series, was canceled.

Rodriguez finished the season in Calgary, where his progress continued. Triple-A pitchers, while often not considered great prospects, usually have far more experience than those in double-A. Rodriguez got plenty of practice hitting curveballs, changeups, and other off-speed pitches, those that often give young players the most trouble. He hit over .300 for Calgary and once again started hitting with power.

The 1994 season had been a learning experience for Rodriguez. He was determined to keep moving ahead.

Chapter Eight:

1995

Minor Problems, Major Dreams

After the season ended, Rodriguez returned home for a few weeks to rest. It had been a busy year for him. Since the beginning of spring training, he hadn't spent more than seven days in a row in the same city. For a while, he was content just to be back home with his family and friends.

But after only a few days, he knew it was time to go to work again. Many of his high school teammates were in the area, back home after playing professionally or attending college. Rodriguez soon began working out with them, either at the Boys and Girls Club or at Westminster, where he was always welcome.

Although many pro baseball players take the

winter off from playing baseball and spend their time resting and working out to prepare for the upcoming season, Alex Rodriguez just wanted to keep playing. When the Mariners asked him if he wanted to play "winter league" baseball, he jumped at the chance.

In the warm-weather islands and nations of the Caribbean such as Puerto Rico, Costa Rica, the Dominican Republic, and even the South American country of Venezuela, professional winter leagues begin play shortly after the major league season ends. Professionals from the American minor and major leagues join talented local players. Many players enjoy returning to their native countries to play before their countrymen.

Winter league baseball isn't like the instructional league. The players take the game seriously and are out to win. The level of talent is very high. Even big major league stars like Texas Ranger catcher Ivan "Pudge" Rodriguez often play in the winter leagues.

Alex Rodriguez returned to the Dominican Republic for the first time since he had moved off the island as a young boy. He joined the Escogido team.

It was a great chance for Rodriguez to keep his skills sharp and face better competition. A lot of the pitchers in the Dominican League had major league experience.

It also gave him the opportunity to speak Spanish all the time, learn more about Dominican life and culture, and reconnect with his roots. He had been living in the United States so long that other Latinos kidded him about his accent and the way he talked!

The high level of competition surprised Rodriguez. He struggled badly and hit only .179. "I was overmatched and my mind really wasn't into it," he admitted later. "I think it woke me up a little bit. I recommend it to every young player."

When Rodriguez returned to the United States for the beginning of spring training in February, major league baseball was still in turmoil. The players and owners hadn't come to an agreement and the players were still not allowed to play.

Major league baseball made plans to open the

season with replacement players, mostly career minor leaguers who would do anything to have a chance to play in the big leagues.

But prospects like Rodriguez were not expected to replace the major leaguers. Everyone knew that the strike would someday be settled, and the major league players' union cautioned the minor leaguers not to participate. If they did, they wouldn't be invited to join the union later. That could affect their careers.

Rodriguez worked out in the Mariners' minor league camp with their triple-A team, which had been transferred from Calgary to Tacoma, Washington, in the offseason. Although some had speculated that he would be the Mariners' shortstop in 1995, given baseball's labor problems, that plan was put on hold.

The plan to use replacement players was a disaster. They weren't very good, and everyone knew it. Finally, just as the season was supposed to start, the players and the union agreed to resume play under the old contract. The start of the season was delayed three weeks, and the season was shortened from 162 games to 144 while the major leaguers held abbreviated spring training and tried to get into shape.

The delay caused the Mariners to change their plans for Rodriguez. They had traded for a second baseman, veteran Joey Cora, and decided to go with two more veterans, Felix Fermin and Luis Sojo, at shortstop. Although they still felt that Rodriguez would soon become their shortstop, they decided he would start the season with Tacoma. If they decided to bring him up to the majors, Tacoma was only a few hundred miles from Seattle.

That's just what happened. After Rodriguez played a couple of games for Tacoma, he was called up to the Mariners in the first week of May when another player was injured.

It was obvious that he had improved. For the first time in the major leagues, he began to display his powerful bat.

But he still struggled at times. In the minors, he hardly ever struck out, but in the major leagues he struck out once every three or four times he came to bat. As one major league manager noted, as of yet Rodriguez "couldn't hit a breaking ball with a big tennis racket." He lunged after curves on the outside corner and usually missed. On May 27, he was sent back to Tacoma.

But the Mariners kept getting hit with the injury bug, as Ken Griffey, Jay Buhner, and Joey Cora were knocked out of the lineup at various times. The Mariners called on Rodriguez to help. He returned to the big leagues only ten days later.

On June 12, 1995, Rodriguez experienced his most memorable day in the big leagues to date. After falling behind Kansas City, 8–1, after two innings, it didn't look as if the Mariners could win.

But Alex keyed a comeback. Coming to bat against veteran pitcher Tom Gordon, a curveball artist, Rodriguez told himself to stay patient and wait for a fastball.

When he got it, he didn't hesitate.

"Crack!" Rodriguez jumped on the pitch and sent it high and deep to the outfield.

This time he didn't stand and admire it, though.

He took off running — hard. Not until he saw the umpire's hand circle through the air did he dare slow down.

It was a home run, the first of his career! Rodriguez was excited, but he didn't celebrate, at least not right away. He kept his head down and jogged quickly around the bases, making sure to touch every one. He didn't want to show up the pitcher.

But when he got to the dugout, he couldn't help himself. As his teammates gave him high-fives, he broke out in a huge grin.

Later in the game, he made a stellar defensive play. On a ground ball up the middle, Rodriguez ranged far to his left.

He stretched out and snagged the ball on the dead run, but his momentum was carrying him toward the outfield. So instead of trying to stop, plant his feet, turn, and throw to first, he just kept going.

Then he spun 360 degrees and threw to first in one motion.

Out! The fans in the Seattle Kingdome roared.

Rodriguez led a remarkable comeback as Seattle

tied the game before finally falling, 10–9. Losing was the only part of the game Rodriguez hadn't enjoyed.

Yet three weeks later, Rodriguez found himself back in the minor leagues.

He accepted the assignment and kept working hard. He was doing great in Tacoma, hitting over .350. Each day, he was getting a little better at hitting the curveball. He knew that was the only thing keeping him from the major leagues. But he was a little frustrated.

The Mariners called him up and sent him back one more time before finally recalling him to Seattle to stay.

It was an exciting time. The Mariners were in a hard-fought battle for the division title with the California Angels and Texas Rangers. Over the last month of the season, only a few games separated the three teams in the standings.

Being in a pennant race was thrilling, but "A-Rod," as his teammates and fans had begun to call him, wasn't playing very much. Manager Lou Piniella decided to go with experience in the pressure of the pennant race. Luis Sojo took over at shortstop. Rodriguez was often used just to pinch-run or pinch-hit late in the game.

The Mariners ended the regular season tied with the California Angels for the division title. They beat the Angels in a one-game playoff to win the right to play the New York Yankees in the first round of the playoffs.

Rodriguez was happy when he learned the Mariners decided to place him on their playoff roster, meaning he was eligible to play. But he knew that unless Sojo was injured, he'd probably spend most of the playoffs on the bench.

He was beginning to get frustrated with his lack of playing time. He even told his mother that he wished he'd attended college instead of deciding to play professional baseball. "I have nothing left to prove at triple-A," he said. "I'd like to stay here [in the majors]. Hopefully, next year I'll have one address."

But everyone on the Mariners knew it would be just a matter of time before Rodriguez made the starting lineup. Even shortstop Luis Sojo admitted,

"He's going to start next year. This guy has so much talent, it's unbelievable. He's got to play. He's like another Ken Griffey Jr."

Just as Rodriguez expected, he sat and watched during the first round of the playoffs, appearing in only one game and getting just one at bat. Still, he had a front-row seat in one of the most exciting play-off series in recent baseball history.

The Yankees and Mariners went at each other inning by inning and pitch by pitch. Ken Griffey cracked five home runs. The Mariners won the series, three games to two. If they could beat Cleveland in the League Championship Series, they would get to go to the World Series.

But the Mariners ran out of steam against Cleveland and lost a hard-fought series to the Indians, four games to two. Rodriguez again appeared in only one game, as a pinch hitter.

When Alex returned to Miami at the end of the season, he embarked on a rigorous physical conditioning program and worked with a nutritionist to get in the best shape of his life. Six days a week, for three hours a day, he worked out with a personal trainer. He also took some special classes with a media consultant to teach him how to talk with the press.

He was determined never to sit on the bench again. He wanted to be ready to be a star.

Chapter Nine:
1996-1997

Starting at the Top

When Alex Rodriguez arrived at spring training, he looked like a new person. He had added pounds of muscle to his body without losing any flexibility or speed. He walked right up to manager Lou Piniella and spoke softly but firmly.

"I'm ready," he said.

Piniella looked him in the eye. He had never seen Rodriguez look so serious.

"I know you are, son."

From the first day of spring training, Rodriguez was the Mariners' starting shortstop. He did nothing to make the club regret that decision.

In the field, he was spectacular, and at the plate, it was as if he had gained ten years of experience over the winter. He was much more patient at the plate and waited for a good pitch to hit. He stopped swinging at curveballs out of the strike zone. And when he did swing at a curveball, instead of trying to pull the pitch, which usually resulted in a weak ground ball, he went with it and hit line drives to right field.

Rodriguez got off to a quick start. One week into the season he opened some eyes when he cracked a home run to dead center field in Tiger Stadium in Detroit, more than 440 feet away. But just a few weeks into the season, with his average nearing .300, he pulled a hamstring muscle and had to sit out more than a dozen games.

If anyone thought the injury would slow Rodriguez down, they were wrong. When he returned to the lineup, he started playing even better than before.

Manager Piniella was impressed. He moved him up in the batting order to the number two spot, right in front of Ken Griffey Jr.

Junior and A-Rod soon became the most feared duo of hitters in baseball. With Griffey hitting behind him, pitchers didn't want to walk Rodriguez, so he got a lot of good pitches to hit. In fact, he got so many hits and was such a threat to steal bases that Griffey got better pitches to hit, too. Pitchers around the league soon began to fear the Mariners.

By mid-June, the youngest player in the American League was among the league leaders in most offensive categories. He was one of the big factors keeping the Mariners in the pennant race.

With Griffey, A-Rod, Jay Buhner, Edgar Martinez, and Tino Martinez in their lineup, the Mariners had plenty of firepower. Their problem was pitching.

Star fastballer Randy Johnson was hurt, and the rest of the Mariner staff was a disaster. Over the course of the season, Piniella eventually used a total of twenty-six pitchers, few of whom did well. In order to win, the Mariners had to score a lot of runs.

A-Rod quickly became one of the most popular players on the team. Attendance went up more than 10,000 fans per game as people turned out in droves to watch the club's high-powered attack. Included in the crowd were often hundreds of young girls who were big Alex Rodriguez fans. As soon as he poked his head out of the dugout, they squealed with delight.

His teammates teased him about his sudden popularity. When he told an interviewer that he hadn't attended his high school prom, he was deluged with thousands of invitations to attend proms in the Seattle area.

Rodriguez handled all the attention as if he were a veteran. Nothing distracted him from his game. He just kept hitting.

Two days before his twenty-first birthday, July 25, 1996, the Mariners rewarded him. They tore up his old contract and gave him another worth ten million dollars over four years.

Unfortunately, the Mariners were unable to match his success. Although they fought hard all year long, they finished second.

But Rodriguez finished first. He led the American League in hitting with an incredible .356 batting average, the highest mark by a right-handed hitter since Joe DeMaggio had hit .381 in 1939. He also led the league in runs scored, total bases, and doubles to go along with 36 home runs and 123 RBIs.

For most players, that would have been a career year. But for Alex Rodriguez, it was just the beginning.

His potential appeared unlimited. At age twenty-one, he was the third youngest batting champion in American League history. Only Al Kaline and Ty Cobb had been younger. Both eventually made the Hall of Fame.

Rodriguez had been looking forward to relaxing in the off-season, but he was asked to go to Japan with a major league all-star team to play a series of exhibitions. Rodriguez didn't want to go at first. Then he found out that Cal Ripken was also a member of the team. He quickly agreed to go.

Even though he was in the major leagues himself, Rodriguez was still a big fan of Ripken. As the team toured Japan, he became good friends with Ripken, and asked his advice about matters both on and off the field. As he said later, Ripken was "everything I thought he would be. We spent time together every day. I learned so much, not just about baseball, but about life. What I learned from Cal is to respect the game, respect the fans. Nothing fancy out there. Just do your job."

Ripken, like everyone in major league baseball, came away impressed with the young star. "He has a chance to be one of the all-time greats," he said.

Rodriguez realized it was important to keep his life in balance. In the off-season he spent nearly as much time working on his mind as he did his game. He began taking some college classes, studying writing and communications. He didn't have to. He just wanted to. "I've always loved learning," he said.

A hitter's second season in the major leagues is often his most difficult. The opposition usually figures out how to pitch a player. The result is the so-called "sophomore slump."

Relatively speaking, Rodriguez was a victim of the slump in 1997, as his production dropped in almost every offensive category. But most other players would have been more than happy to have played as well as he did, as he still hit .300 and remained one of the most dangerous hitters in the league. He also accomplished one of baseball's rarest feats.

It happened in Detroit as the Mariners played the Tigers. In the first inning, Rodriguez cracked a home run. In his next at bat, he singled, and in the eighth inning he tripled.

He came up in the ninth inning needing only a double to hit for what is known as the "cycle" — a single, double, triple, and home run all in the same game.

Pitcher Doug Brocail worked him carefully. He tried to sneak a fastball past Rodriguez inside.

Alex fought the pitch off, hitting it the opposite way, toward right field, in what he later described as a "jam shot, a sand wedge." The ball fell fair and rolled down the line.

At first, Rodriguez wasn't even thinking of going for a double — the Mariners had a big lead and he didn't want to show up the pitcher.

But as he neared first base, his coach, aware that Rodriguez needed only a double for the cycle, waved his arms and yelled, "Go, go, go!" He knew the cycle is such a rarity that the other team wouldn't think Rodriguez was showing them up. A-Rod kicked it into high gear and made it to second base.

True to form, Rodriguez then took the accomplishment in stride. "To me, the win was the most exciting part," he said.

There was plenty of excitement the rest of the season, as the Mariners made winning a regular occurrence. Seattle was one of the best teams in baseball. Randy Johnson returned to lead the pitching staff, winning 20 games and striking out as many as 19 hitters in one game. And Ken Griffey Jr. threatened to break Roger Maris's single-season home run record of 61 before finishing with 56. The team set a major league record with 264 home runs and romped to the A.L. West title, winning a club record 90 games.

They won the right to play Baltimore in the division championship series. Cal Ripken played for Baltimore, and Rodriguez was excited to have the opportunity to play against his hero in such a meaningful set of games. In fact, when Rodriguez had finally moved into his own home, he'd taken the poster of Ripken that hung over his bed with him. He had it framed and put in a place of honor in his new home.

Ripken put on a clinic in the series, hitting .438, better than any other regular player. Although the Mariners played hard, nearly the entire team went into a batting slump. Griffey, Jay Buhner, and Edgar Martinez hit a collective .182. Without much run support, Randy Johnson, who'd lost only five times during the regular season, lost both games he pitched against the Orioles. Baltimore won the series, three games to one.

Of all the Mariners, Rodriguez played the best, hitting .313 and cracking a home run in game one. But he was still disappointed in the end result. Personal success meant little to him when his team didn't win.

Over the next few years, that would determine his future.

Chapter Ten:
1998–2000

$252 Million Dollar Man

Rodriguez and his teammates looked forward to making an appearance in the postseason an annual event. But A-Rod knew he wouldn't be satisfied with anything less than a World Series ring. His good friend, Derek Jeter, had already won a ring with the world champion 1996 New York Yankees. Rodriguez wanted one, too.

Entering the 1998 season, the Mariners appeared on track to reach that goal. In Randy Johnson, Griffey, and A-Rod, three of the best players in baseball, the Mariners had a strong nucleus. The team was in the process of building a beautiful new ballpark, and they enjoyed impressive fan support.

But in 1998, Mariner fans began to grow impatient.

Once again, their pitching collapsed, particularly their bullpen. Time and time again, the Mariners took a lead late into a ball game only to lose it. It didn't matter that both Rodriguez and Griffey were enjoying spectacular years. The Mariners just couldn't win.

The team knew that within the next two years, Johnson, Griffey, and Rodriguez would all be up for new contracts. The ball club didn't think they'd be able to afford all three players. They'd soon have to decide whom to keep.

Randy Johnson made one decision easy for them. He became frustrated with the organization and the Mariner bullpen and made it clear that he wanted to be traded. Late in the season, he was sent to the Houston Astros in exchange for some young prospects.

A-Rod understood why the trade happened, but he still wasn't pleased. Without Johnson to anchor the pitching staff, he knew the Mariners would have little chance to win.

The team had other problems as well. With both

Griffey and Rodriguez competing for the spotlight, there was a measure of jealousy between the two players.

When Rodriguez had first joined the Mariners, Griffey had been one of the first players to befriend him. But over the past few seasons, they had slowly grown apart. Griffey, after all, was several years older and married with a family of his own. A-Rod was still a young man and single. They didn't have much in common anymore. Both were still doing their best to win, but each was very competitive and wanted to be the best player in the game. And both players knew the Mariners probably wouldn't be able to afford to keep both of them in Seattle. They were also growing frustrated with losing.

Meanwhile, all of baseball focused on the record-setting home run race between Mark McGwire, Sammy Sosa, and Ken Griffey Jr. While those three fought it out, Rodriguez quietly put together one of the greatest seasons a shortstop has ever had. Once again, he was among the league leaders in most offensive categories. And with 42 home runs and 46 stolen bases, he became only the third player ever to join the so-called "40-40" club. Even Ken Griffey Jr. hadn't done that.

In the off-season, Rodriguez started the Alex Rodriguez Foundation, a charity to help children. He also contributed to the Boys and Girls Club in Miami and sponsored an educational program for kids in Seattle. Helping people is important to him.

Few observers expected much from the Mariners in 1999. They simply didn't have enough pitching to compete.

What little chance the team had to win evaporated only two games into the season. Rodriguez twisted his left knee and tore some cartilage.

A few decades ago, an injury like torn knee cartilage likely would have ended a player's season. But today, due to some advances in surgical techniques, doctors can operate on the knee through a tiny hole. Recovery is measured in a matter of weeks instead of months. Two days after injuring the knee, Rodriguez had surgery. He returned to the lineup less than six weeks later.

He cracked a home run in his first at bat after returning, but the Mariners were already dropping out of the race. All their fans had to look forward to was the opening of their new ballpark, Safeco Field.

When the ballpark was being designed, the Mariners claimed that it would increase the amount of money the team would make and help them afford to keep players like Griffey and Rodriguez. But the park had run way over budget, and the team was responsible for the extra costs. Now it appeared as if the ballpark would actually *prevent* them from signing both players.

Although fans loved the new park, which featured an open-air roof that protected the field while still giving the park an outdoor feel, Griffey and Rodriguez were less than pleased. The Kingdome had been small, and a good park in which to hit home runs. But in the new park, the fences were more distant. Both players would have a tougher time hitting home runs there.

Still, despite missing over thirty games, Rodriguez managed to match his career high with 42 home runs. He was still getting better. Had he not been hurt, he probably would have had his greatest season.

In the off-season, Ken Griffey turned down a huge contract offer from the Mariners and requested a trade. He was dealt to the Cincinnati Reds.

All of a sudden, Alex Rodriguez was considered the Mariners' leader and was their only big star. At the same time, he had to start worrying about his own future. His contract was due to expire at the end of the 2000 season, at which time he could become a free agent, free to sign with any team in baseball.

Some observers wondered if Rodriguez would continue to be as productive without Griffey in the lineup. Few expected the Mariners to play very well.

But the pitching prospects they had received in the Randy Johnson trade had matured and were ready to contribute. A couple of other trades the team made worked out, and suddenly the Mariners had the best pitching they'd had in years.

That made all the difference. Well, that and Alex Rodriguez.

He silenced his critics with the best season so far, setting career highs in virtually every category but home runs and batting average despite missing two weeks with a concussion and a knee injury. He even improved in the field, committing only eight errors for the season, an incredibly small number for a shortstop. He was a true team leader, as he made everyone on the team better and provided a calming presence on the field.

The Mariners surprised everyone by playing well. "We're having a blast," said A-Rod as the season began to wind down with the Mariners still in the playoff hunt. "Everybody feels like we're one-twenty-fifth of a major project. We're not a bunch of stars."

The Mariners fought the Oakland A's for the division title right down to the last day of the season. The A's edged them out for the title, but Seattle still qualified for the wild-card spot in the playoffs.

In the first round, the Mariners faced the Chicago

White Sox. Seattle's pitching dominated the series, shutting down White Sox hitting star Frank Thomas. The Mariners swept Chicago in three straight games to earn the right to play the New York Yankees for the American League pennant.

"I would like to write a book about every single person in this clubhouse," said Rodriguez after.

Rodriguez knew he would have to play better against New York. He hadn't hit very well against Chicago. The Yankees were two-time defending champions. He knew he would have to play his best to beat them.

Everything went according to plan in the first game. Pitcher Freddy Garcia didn't give up a run, and the Mariners took a 1–0 lead into the sixth inning.

A-Rod came to bat with no one on base against New York pitcher Denny Neagle. Neagle pitched carefully, and Rodriguez fouled back a change-up on a 3–1 count to make it 3–2.

Neagle admitted later that he should have thrown another change-up. Instead, he threw a fastball.

"Crack!" The ball soared high and deep to left field, ricocheting off the foul pole for a home run. Seattle led, 2–0.

"The whole at bat I was focused on a fastball in, and I finally got it," said Rodriguez later. The Mariners hung on to win, 2–1.

But that was about the only highlight for the Mariners. The Yankees swept the next three games and eventually won the series in six games. Rodriguez had played well, but the Mariners bullpen had folded before the Yankees.

As Rodriguez packed his locker at the end of the season and took off his Mariner uniform, he knew it might be for the last time. He was still up in the air about re-signing with Seattle. In fact, he planned to listen to offers from other teams.

Never before had a player as young and talented as Rodriguez been available on the free-agent market. Everyone expected him to receive the most lucrative contract in baseball history. The only question became which team would sign him.

Most observers expected the New York Mets and

Los Angeles Dodgers to be most interested, but those teams announced that they had decided not to pursue him. They didn't want to spend the money. Then the Braves and Yankees passed, and the Mariners dropped out of the bidding.

The White Sox and Texas Rangers were the only two teams willing to meet the 200-million-dollar bid A-rod's agent, Scott Boras, told teams to be prepared to pay.

The White Sox soon dropped out. The Rangers' new owner, Tom Hicks, wanted Rodriguez badly. Finally, after weeks of negotiations, the two sides agreed to a ten-year contract worth an incredible 252 million dollars!

Even Rodriguez admitted, "I'm almost embarrassed and ashamed of this contract. Here I am, all my life I've enjoyed playing the role of the underdog and all of a sudden I have this two-hundred-fifty-two tag over my head." Others found it shocking. But Hicks summed it up by saying, "If there's a player deserving of the largest contract in baseball, it's this player."

He might be right. Alex Rodriguez, at age twenty-five, has already reached a level of success most players only dream of. Yet he has never forgotten where he came from. Baseball makes him happier than anything else in the world.

At heart, he is still the little boy in the *monte,* playing the game he loves.

Chapter Eleven:
2001–2003

Lone Ranger

After signing such a big contract, Alex Rodriguez heeded the words of Ken Griffey Jr. Several years earlier his old teammate had also signed a big free agent contract. He told Rodriguez that now fans expected him to earn his money.

"Griffey got a message to me that I was in for my most challenging year," said Rodriguez later. "That's why I worked so hard over the winter." Rodriguez worked out at the gym more than ever before in the off season. He also turned down several offers to appear on television and elsewhere. He didn't want anything to distract him from the start of the season.

He also knew that, as the highest-paid and best-known Latino athlete in the United States, many people would be looking up to him. "I know what I mean to all Latinos," he said. He didn't want to let anyone down.

Team owner Tom Hicks was also doing his best not to let Rodriguez down. He told his new star player that despite signing Rodriguez to such a big contract, he still had plenty of money to spend on other players. Hicks wanted the Rangers to win a world championship. He promised A-Rod that nothing would stop the team from reaching that goal. And he seemed good for his promise; after all, he had already taken the Dallas Stars of the National Hockey League and built them into Stanley Cup champions. He expected to do the same with the Rangers.

The Rangers were known as a team of big hitters, and Rodriguez certainly added to that reputation. His teammates on Texas included All-Star catcher Ivan "Pudge" Rodriguez, who had hit .347 in 2000, and first baseman Rafael Palmiero, one of the best home run hitters in the game. The Rangers had never had much of a problem scoring runs, and with Alex Rodriguez on board, they looked to be even more powerful at bat.

The Rangers' problem had always been pitching.

In the 2000 season their pitching was awful and the club finished 71-91, in last place in the National League West. And now their best pitcher, closer John Wetteland, had retired.

Hicks knew that in order to build a winning team, he needed a new rotation on the mound. But unfortunately, he couldn't persuade any star pitchers to sign with the Rangers. To compensate, he kept acquiring more hitters, like DH Andres Gallaraga and third baseman Ken Caminiti, a former MVP in the National League. The Rangers opened the 2001 season with plenty of firepower, but not much pitching.

For opening day they traveled to San Juan, Puerto Rico, to play the Toronto Blue Jays. Major League Baseball wanted to become more popular in Latin America and had decided to play the game in Puerto Rico to showcase Latino stars like Rodriguez and others on the Blue Jays and Rangers.

Rodriguez was confident before the game, but still nervous. He knew that everyone was watching to see how well he would play in his first game in a Texas uniform.

He got off to a quick start. In the first inning, batting third, he laced a base hit, his first as a Ranger. A moment later Rafael Palmeiro cracked a double, and Rodriguez raced home to score the Rangers' first run of the game.

Unfortunately, that would be the last run the Rangers would score and also the highlight of Alex Rodriguez's first day as a Ranger. The rest of the day would be a disaster.

The first ball hit to him was a routine ground ball. He fielded it perfectly and tossed the ball to first base just as he had done countless times before. He saw the first baseman reach for the ball, and then keep reaching. Rodriguez had thrown the ball into the stands for an error! The fans jeered.

A short time later, while trying to turn a double play, he slipped and fell. The crowd booed again. But the worst was still to come. Later in the game, with a runner on first, he glided over to field a ground ball and make the throw to second. He fielded the ball cleanly, but as he shuffled his feet to make the throw, the spikes on one of his shoes got tangled with his shoelaces. He fell face first to the ground. As the crowd laughed, he wanted to crawl under second base. He had never felt so embarrassed in his life.

The Rangers went on to lose, 8-1. Rodriguez knew he had played a lousy game, but he didn't make any excuses. "You have to start somewhere," he said later. "Today had a little bit of everything." Luckily, that day of errors proved to be a fluke. Before long, he was again performing to his usual standard, making great plays and hitting home runs.

Unfortunately, the Rangers as a whole were terrible. In late April and early May they lost eleven out of twelve games. At the same time, Rodriguez's old team, the Mariners, got off to a fabulous start, one of the best in baseball history. By the second week of May the Rangers were already in last place, fourteen games behind the Mariners.

To the disappointment of Ranger fans, it didn't get any better. As the season progressed, the Rangers fell further and further behind in the division race. They simply didn't have enough good pitching to compete.

But you'd have never known that the Rangers had no chance to reach the playoffs by the way Rodriguez played. Every day he went out onto the field and battled as if it were the last game of the World Series. "Alex has played tremendously well," said teammate Gabe Kapler. "We've gotten everything we could have possibly hoped for from Alex Rodriguez." Added one major league scout, "His team scuffled but he still dived for balls even when his team was down 10–1. He plays hard all the time. He plays the game right."

Even though the Rangers finished the season with a disappointing record of 73-89, dead last in the AL West, Rodriguez had the best season of his career. He cracked 52 home runs and 135 RBIs to go with his .318 batting average. But his old club, the Mariners, won an incredible 116 games to take the division and make the playoffs. Rodriguez could only watch.

In 2002, owner Tom Hicks seemed better prepared to make good on his promise to acquire more pitching. In the off season he signed several hurlers, including Los Angeles Dodger star Chan Ho Park, starters Ismael Valdes and Dave Burba, and reliever Todd Van Poppel. The Rangers also re-signed slugging outfielder Juan Gonzalez to a two-year deal.

Entering the season, Rodriguez was certain that the Rangers would be able to compete. Although he realized it might not be possible for them to catch the Mariners, the Rangers hoped to make a run at the wild card spot.

Yet for the second season in a row, the Rangers got off to an awful start. None of their new pitchers threw as well as expected. On May 25 the team fell into fourth place, and they stayed there for the rest of the season, finishing with a record of 72–90.

But despite the losing season, Rodriguez played even better. This time he hit 57 home runs, the second highest total for a right-handed hitter in American League history, behind only Roger Maris's record of 61 in 1961. He also hit .300 and drove in 142 runs. But as one baseball executive commented, hardly anyone noticed. "He's the best player in the game," said the executive, "and it feels like nobody even talks about him." The fans seemed to forget about him completely. He finished second in American League MVP votes, behind Oakland Athletics shortstop Miguel Tejada. The difference seemed to be that the A's had made the playoffs, while the Rangers had not come close.

Rodriguez tried to put the year behind him. In the off-season, he married his longtime fiancée Cynthia Scurtis and tried to look ahead to the 2003 season. The Rangers fired manager Jerry Narron and hired former Yankee and Arizona manager Buck Showalter. And for the second season in a row, owner Tom Hicks tried to acquire some pitching help, signing closer Ugueth Urbina, Esteban Yan, and several others. Entering spring training, Rodriguez was once again optimistic.

Then disaster struck. A few weeks into spring training, Rodriguez suffered a herniated disk in his neck, the first serious injury of his career. Fortunately, he had to sit out for less than a month. He still managed to make the opening day lineup, but the injury caused him to look upon his career from a new perspective. Now he realized his time as a major league ballplayer could end in an instant. With this in mind, he entered the season determined to win.

On April 2, he cracked the 300th home run of his career, making the record books as the youngest player in baseball history to hit so many home runs. If he could maintain his pace for another ten or twelve years, he would have a good shot at breaking the all-time home run record currently held by Henry "Hank" Aaron with 756.

But Rodriguez didn't care about records. He just wanted to win games. Yet the Rangers were still struggling and by the end of May it was obvious that they were on their way to another fourth place finish in the AL West with a record well under .500.

Owner Tom Hicks decided to change course and rebuild. He began trading away the Rangers' high-priced players and announced that he would give some rookies a chance.

Rodriguez knew that grooming young players to be champions could take years, which meant it could be years before the Rangers would be a championship team. The prospect didn't please him. Nevertheless, he still played his usual superb game. As the Rangers stumbled to another 71-91 record,

Rodriguez was about the only player on the team not to suffer a letdown. He finished with 47 home runs and 118 RBIs.

But it was clear to baseball fans that he was becoming frustrated. On November 18, 2003, he was named the Most Valuable Player in the American League, beating out Carlos Delgado of the Toronto Blue Jays. But when Rodriguez spoke to reporters after winning the award, he didn't sound very happy. Although he said he felt "humbled and overwhelmed," he also admitted that even though he had a clause in his contract that prevented the Rangers from trading him, he would "definitely" approve a trade if it enabled him to go to a winning team.

It didn't take long for another team to try to take him up on his offer. The Boston Red Sox had just suffered a crushing defeat to the Yankees in the seventh game of the ALCS. They offered to swap stars with the Rangers, sending outfielder Manny Ramirez to the Rangers for Rodriguez.

For the Rangers, the trade made sense. Hicks was having financial trouble, and although Ramirez earned nearly twenty million dollars a year, his contract was shorter. In the long run the Rangers would save nearly 100 million dollars in the deal.

The trade excited all of baseball. The Red Sox thought Rodriguez could finally help them win a world championship, and Major League Baseball believed that having Rodriguez in a hot baseball town like Boston would be good for the game. Commissioner Bud Selig even suspended some rules and allowed the Red Sox to negotiate with Rodriguez before a deal was made. Even though they were desperate to acquire him, Boston wanted to restructure his contract.

Rodriguez was definitely interested in joining the Red Sox. His wife had many relatives in the Boston area, and he loved the idea of playing in Fenway Park, where every game felt like a playoff game. He knew that if he could lead the Red Sox to a world championship — their first since 1918 — he would be a hero in New England forever.

But as it turned out, Boston wasn't the only team interested in Rodriguez. In early February of 2004, the New York Yankees contacted the Rangers to make an offer. Negotiations followed. Then, a little less than two weeks later, the deal was made and approved by MLB commissioner Bud Selig. Alex Rodriguez would become a Yankee.

The baseball world was stunned. Red Sox fans were in an uproar, claiming they had been robbed. But the truth of the matter was that the Yankees made Rodriguez and the Rangers a deal they couldn't pass up. George Steinbrenner, the owner of the Yankees, was willing to give up two of his players and to pay top dollar — the most ever in major league history, in fact — to get Rodriguez. The Red Sox and other teams simply couldn't meet or beat the offer.

For Rodriguez, being a Yankee meant making a few changes. For one, he would no longer be playing the position he'd played for years. The Yankees already have a star shortstop in Derek Jeter, so Rodriguez would move to third base. And because the Yankees retired uniform number three, Babe Ruth's number, A-Rod would now be wearing number 13.

But such changes haven't seemed to faze the star player. Instead, he has his eye on the ultimate baseball prize, winning the World Series, something he believes might not have happened if he had stayed with the Rangers.

"The bigger challenge is staying south," Rodriguez said during spring training in 2004. "Was [a championship] realistic? Probably not. One thing about [Rangers owner] Tom Hicks: He gave it a heckuva try. I'd rather try and come up short than not try at all."

Still, he couldn't contain his enthusiasm for the trade. "It's so much larger than life. It's too good to be true."

For Alex Rodriguez, a player whose abilities are larger than life, the future itself looks very bright indeed.

Chapter 12:
2004–2005

A-Rod in Pinstripes

Alex Rodriguez wasn't fazed by the change of position or uniform number. He had his eye on much bigger things, specifically, helping his new team with the World Series.

He took to the field in a Yankee uniform for the first time on March 30, 2004. Fans were eager to see what the highest paid player in the major leagues could do. Although he struck out swinging his first two at bats, in the sixth inning he doubled to deep right, and then scored on a double from Gary Sheffield to put the Yankees ahead 3–2 over the Tampa Bay Devil Rays.

Unfortunately, that was the last run the Yankees scored that night. They dropped their season opener to the Devil Rays 8–3. They made up for the loss the next night, however, by trouncing Tampa Bay 12–1.

A-Rod worked hard, but through April managed to pound in only four home runs in eighty-two at bats. Still, he was helping the team with his base stealing and his ability to get on base. At the end of April he started a two-month long streak league leading in both categories.

The Yankees, meanwhile, were busy chalking up win after win. By the All-Star break on July 13, they were several games ahead of the next closest team, their archrivals, the Boston Red Sox. When the two teams met for the first of a three game series on July 23, New York's record was 61–34 while Boston was 52–44. Still, those numbers didn't reflect the fact that the Sox had won six of their past eight outings.

The July 23 game was played in Boston before fans hungry for a win. They hoped they might also see Alex Rodriguez, the player they had once coveted, continue his poor showing against the Red Sox pitchers. But he turned things around and in the eighth inning, slugged a single that scored the winning run, giving New York an 8–7 victory.

The next day saw rain soaking Fenway Park, and the second New York-Boston game was postponed for an hour. Both teams went scoreless and hitless in the first inning. Then, at the top of the second, Rodriguez belted an infield single that he stretched into a double. He advanced to third on the next hit and then scored on a double by Hideki Matsui. New York scored again before the end of the inning.

Going into the third inning, the score was still Yankees 2, Red Sox 0. Bernie Williams came to the plate and smacked a double. Then Derek Jeter singled, sending Williams to third.

With two men on base, the Sox needed to make an out. They made two on a double play from second to first that saw batter Gary Sheffield returning to the dugout along with Jeter. Williams scored, however, giving the Yankees a three run lead.

Next up was Alex Rodriguez. Arroyo threw.

Whap!

The sound wasn't bat hitting ball, it was ball hitting elbow — A-Rod's left elbow. The third baseman grimaced and then stared long and hard at the pitcher before starting down the base path to first. Then, unable to control his anger at being hit, he began shouting at Arroyo.

Catcher Jason Varitek immediately stood up and confronted him.

"They started to cuss each other," recalled umpire Bruce Froemming later, "and that was it."

Varitek and Rodriguez got into a shouting match, with the catcher yelling for the third baseman to get to first base. Suddenly, Varitek shoved his glove in Rodriguez's face — and the dugouts of both teams emptied for an all-out brawl that ended with four players, including A-Rod and Varitek, being ejected.

The Sox took that game as well as the next one to draw ever closer to the Yankees in the standings. At the season's end, New York's record was 101–61 and Boston's was 98–64. Boston knocked off the Angels and New York dispatched the Twins in the divisional playoffs.

Now the Yankees and the Red Sox were set to battle it out for the American League pennant. That race ended up being one for the history books.

Game one was played at Yankee Stadium on October 12. By the night's end, Boston fans were silent, struck dumb by a 10–7 loss. Game two found them even quieter after the Yankees again emerged victorious, 3–1. Game three was scheduled to take place at Fenway on October 15, but was postponed for a day due to rain.

Alex Rodriguez had been helpful during the first two games but not really a standout. That changed in game three. In his first at bat he doubled to left field, sending Derek Jeter home to put the Yankees on the scoreboard. Then A-Rod crossed home plate on a home run by Hideki Matsui. By the end of the first inning New York led 3–0.

But Boston responded in the second inning with four runs of their own to go up by one.

Rodriguez was the lead off batter at the top of the third. Arroyo threw and *whack!* A-Rod sent the ball soaring for a home run. It was four all — then with Ramiro Mendoza in for Arroyo, it became 6–4.

Boston wasn't beaten yet, however. They pounded out a series of hits that tied the game going into the top of the fourth.

Unfortunately for Boston fans, things quickly got out of hand after that. While the Red Sox had a re-volving door on the mound, replacing pitcher after pitcher, the Yankees chalked up run after run until by the game's end, the score was an unbelievable 19–8.

By the end of this rout, most people believed the Red Sox had no chance of advancing to the World Series; they would have to win the remaining four games. No team in the history of baseball had ever overcome a three game deficit

Midway through game four, it looked as though Boston would indeed be swept. A two-run homer by Alex Rodriguez in the third inning put the Yankees ahead 2–0. That score stuck until the fifth inning, when Boston finally got on the board with three runs. New York answered with two more of their own at the top of the sixth. It was Yankees 4, Sox 3.

Boston tried to score in the sixth, seventh, and eighth but couldn't get a man on. New York continued to hold their one run lead. Then, in the middle of the bottom of the ninth, Red Sox outfielder Dave Roberts got on first. Then he stole second. And then he raced home on a single hit by Bill Mueller.

The game went into extra innings. Finally, in the bottom of the twelfth, Manny Ramirez of the Red Sox singled. David Ortiz strode to the plate and blasted a pitch hurled by Paul Quantrill for a two-run homer to give Boston their first win of the series.

At the next day's game, Boston got on the scoreboard first, toting up two runs in the first inning. New York came back in the second with one, then added three more in the sixth to take a two run lead. But the Sox added two of their own in the eighth to knot the score at 4–4. Finally, in the fourteenth inning, after nearly six hours of play, David Ortiz once again pushed the Sox over with a blooper to the infield that scored Johnny Damon.

Suddenly, the series stood at New York 3 games, Boston 2.

The series moved back to New York for game six. New York was still favored to win, but the Red Sox were fired up by their two wins and were not to be denied.

The game was scoreless until the fourth inning, when the Sox put four runs on the board thanks to an RBI by Jason Varitek and a three-run homer by Mark Bellhorn. Curt Schilling was on the mound for the Sox and despite a painful and observably bloody ankle, knocked down batter after batter until Bernie

Williams managed to clock a homer in the bottom of the seventh. Schilling pitched the remainder of the inning and then was relieved by Bronson Arroyo.

Arroyo struck out Tony Clark then gave up a double to Miguel Cairo. Derek Jeter followed with a single that scored Cairo. With one out and Jeter on first, Alex Rodriguez came to the plate.

Since the July fracas, there had been no love lost between Rodriguez and Arroyo. Rodriguez tapped out a hit that bounded between the pitcher's mound and first base. Arroyo scooped up the ball and ran hard for first.

A-Rod was close to the base. As Arroyo drew near, Rodriguez reached out and slapped the ball from the pitcher's glove. The ball bounced away down the right-field line. Jeter rounded the bases and crossed home plate.

Meanwhile, Red Sox manager Terry Francona roared out of the dugout to argue the incident with the umpires. After a few minutes of huddled discussion, the umpires called Jeter back to first, ruling Rodriguez's glove slap illegal.

Rodriguez was infuriated at the call, but there was

nothing he could do about it. There was nothing he could do about the game's final score either: Red Sox 4, Yankees 2. The series was all tied up at three games apiece.

The next night, before a crowd of 56,129 fans in Yankee Stadium, the Red Sox made history by winning game seven, the first time any team has ever come from behind to take four games in a row to win the pennant.

Alex Rodriguez was bitterly disappointed. "I'm embarrassed right now," he said after the loss. "Obviously, that hurts, watching them on our field celebrating."

Despite the defeat, A-Rod had had a strong first year with the Yankees. He had slugged in thirty-six home runs, 106 RBIs, and posted a .286 average. When he showed up at spring training in 2005, he had added several pounds of muscle to his frame, muscle that he put to good use early on.

Three weeks into the season, he had one of the best games of his career. In a 12–4 rout of the Angels, he socked in three home runs and ten RBIs in just five at bats.

"Definitely tonight was one of those magical nights," he said after the game.

On May 4, he posted his tenth homer of the season to put him at the top of league in that category. He still led the league at the end of the month, with sixteen, and in RBIs as well with forty-six, earning him the AL Player of the Month award.

June saw him racking up his 400th career home run. At 29 years, 316 days old he was the youngest player in the Major Leagues to reach that benchmark. In mid-July, just shy of this thirtieth birthday, he had more home runs and RBIs than Hank Aaron, more runs than Rickey Henderson, and more hits than Pete Rose had had in their twenties. That same month, he was voted to the play in the All-Star game for the ninth year in a row and shortly after logged a game-winning two-run homer off a Curt Schilling pitch. That win was particularly sweet as the Sox and the Yankees were neck-and-neck in the standings. However, this year they were battling for second place behind the surprising Chicago White Sox, who by the end of July had a healthy lead on both teams.

In mid-August Rodriguez set yet another record

when he passed Joe DiMaggio and Garry Sheffield as the player who had the greatest number of home runs hit in a single season by a right hander at Yankee Stadium. And on September 15, he fired in his 42nd home run of the year in a win against the Devil Rays. That victory put his team as close to first place as they had been all year.

"The team is playing with a lot of urgency right now," Rodriguez commented after the win. "We realize how important each game is, and we're taking this as our playoff."

Where the Yankees end up in 2005 remains to be seen, but one thing appears certain. If Alex Rodriguez continues to post the kind of numbers he has this season — 42 home runs, 114 RBIs, and 174 hits in 544 at bats for an average of .320 — he will be making Yankee fans happy for many years to come.

The #1
Sports Series
for Kids

MATT CHRISTOPHER®

Read them all!

*Previously published as Crackerjack Halfback

All available in paperback from Little, Brown and Company

**Previously published as Pressure Play

Matt Christopher®

Muhammad Ali	Tara Lipinski
Lance Armstrong	Mark McGwire
Kobe Bryant	Yao Ming
Jennifer Capriati	Shaquille O'Neal
Jeff Gordon	Jackie Robinson
Ken Griffey Jr.	Alex Rodriguez
Mia Hamm	Babe Ruth
Tony Hawk	Curt Schilling
Ichiro	Sammy Sosa
Derek Jeter	Venus and Serena Williams
Randy Johnson	Tiger Woods
Michael Jordan	
Mario Lemieux	